A NEW MOD

LEADING BEYOND YOUR LIMITS

MICHAEL MURPHY

DEVOTIONAL INSIGHT FROM VALERIE MURPHY

VIDE

VIDE

Vide Press
6200 Second Street
Washington D.C. 20011
www.VidePress.com

ISBN 978-1-7351814-3-1

Printed in the United States of America

Dedication

We dedicate this book to our children and their families, who know well our limitations.

Our prayer is that they have an ever-deepening knowledge that God is faithful, faithful, faithful, and His Word is living and true! Along this journey of the ups and downs of faith, God moves us beyond limits and gives us access to the unlimited nature of His Kingdom.

Acknowledgments

We would like to acknowledge Danica Gebru and Jesse Darrow for their much-needed feedback and assistance with our early and late manuscripts. Their input has been immensely valuable.

We also want to share our appreciation for specific individuals who have impacted our personal faith journeys. These include Eric Johnson, Larry Crabb, Ruth Haley Barton, and those others who have touched our lives deeply. We are thankful for the Lord working through all of you to build up the Name and Body of Christ! All things point to the glory of God!

Table of Contents

Preface

Writing a book on leadership in the Church is an intimidating thing, yet we are compelled to approach the task. What qualifies someone to write such a thing, and what gives a person the confidence that what he or she is writing is of any generalized value? Also, "leadership" is defined in so many different ways, and it can be very difficult to focus on a specific area.

Yet, in our roles as church leaders and counselors, we have seen too many injured people over the years who feel excluded or outcast by the very organizations that should be the most welcoming to them. Feelings we have heard expressed are those of not fitting or not being accepted, or of being judged, condemned, or simply ignored. At other times, we have seen excited new believers fade and disappear as their enthusiasm falls on deaf or jaded ears. We have seen hungry hearts starve for education that fills the soul. We have seen disillusionment labeled as sin instead of growth. We have seen mature believers turned away because they do not fit the vision of the organization. Our hearts hurt over this, and we simply cannot remain silent.

This failure to be the Body of Christ to the hurting and wounded in our world is a clear failure of leadership. It is our sincere belief that this failure is not one of intent, but one of misunderstanding. Leadership in the church that Christ desires is a countercultural leadership that honors the dignity of all those whom God loves. That makes leadership within the Body of Christ something that is very different from much of what the world teaches on leadership.

We are convinced that the strategic model of business leadership, while valuable in part, is not an appropriate model of leadership for the central work of the church. A new model of leadership is needed in our churches, and we pray that this book may spark some thoughts, introspections, discussions, and movement in the development of that new model. The reflections at the end of each chapter are designed to assist you in applying the content of each chapter to your own life and ministry setting. Prayerfully approaching these sections will bring insight and understanding beyond our limits as the authors.

Chapter 1:

What Is Church Leadership?

Maybe the best place to start is to talk about how we see leadership. Leadership is a topic that can be understood in many different ways, and the way it is understood will influence how one both speaks and hears anything communicated about leadership. How we understand leadership greatly influences what we say about it.

For many, church leadership is limited to those who are on paid staff and the designated elders. Others may expand that to include key volunteer leaders. Leadership guidance for these is focused on how one motivates and inspires others to adopt the vision and strategy of the leader. There are numerous books and training programs that approach leadership in this light. This book is not one of these.

Leadership built on this premise is fundamentally limited by the limitations of those who cast the vision. John Maxwell[1] called this the "law of the lid." By this he meant that no follower of a vision can rise above the topmost point set by the vision caster. Leadership then becomes an innate or learned ability that determines the effectiveness of the accomplishment of any given vision. And Maxwell is correct in his assessment, when we understand that from his point of view, leadership is about getting people to follow a vision that is well thought out, strategically implemented, and sound in principle.

1 Maxwell, 1998

Another author of leadership principles, Steven B. Sample, talks about the requirements of leadership. In his book, *The Contrarian's Guide to Leadership*,[2] Sample speaks of the need to sell oneself before selling the vision. In this context, his point is that a leader is about credibility, and the vision or direction of leadership is secondary. He cites a number of very public examples, both successful and unsuccessful, to make his point. Again, like Maxwell, he is absolutely on target if we are talking about a purely strategic goal of accomplishing a task.

Leadership in the church, however, is a significantly different thing. We believe that the very best leaders in the church are followers, first and foremost. A church leader is a divinely called individual whom God has ordained, and a congregation has confirmed to act as a catalyst to accomplish a goal that is beyond the natural or learned abilities of that individual. There are numerous examples of these types of leaders, some leading large visions, some leading small visions. It is not the size of the goal that matters, but simply the source of the call. If the call is of God, the goal is worth pursuing and pursuing diligently.

Let's consider one such example. We find him in the book of Exodus.[3] His name is Moses. God called Moses to deliver His people out of bondage in Egypt. What an honor! We would expect that Moses would be leaping within his soul that his God would find him so worthy. Instead, we read about his argument with God. Moses put before God every possible reason that He should choose someone else for this honor, until he made God angry. Only then did Moses bow in submission and move in obedience. Yet, God did not consider that Moses' inability to speak well was an impediment to his speaking for God himself. What a "lid" to overcome!

If we are to understand the teaching of how God selects His leaders, we might suspect that reluctance is a primary prerequisite. Gideon, in the book of Judges,[4] tested the call of God twice by throwing his fleece outside overnight, first asking for it to be wet when the ground was dry, and then dry when the ground was wet. Even the great King

---

[2] Sample, 2002

[3] Exodus, chapters 3–4

[4] Judges 6:36–40

David refrained from seizing his anointed role from Saul for more than twenty years.[5]

We believe that the very best leaders in the church are followers, first and foremost.

Dan Allender understands this difference very well. In his book, *Leading with a Limp,*[6] Allender claims that flight is the only sane response to God's call to leadership. This is a very different picture from what we generally expect of our trained professional leaders in the Church. We tend to expect our leaders to be confident, assured of the vision God has given them and unencumbered by doubt and insecurity. After all, hasn't God given them the vision?

If we are to understand the teaching of how God selects His leaders, we might suspect that reluctance is a primary prerequisite.

But what person, except an egomaniac, could be self-assured of accomplishing a vision as big as God's? When we receive a call from God, it invariably involves stretching us beyond our known abilities and forces us to face the very real prospect of imminent and very public failure. He calls us to tasks that truly involve the life and death of the soul, for both ourselves and those He calls to lead. When we grasp the magnitude of the responsibility that God is willing to delegate to us, it literally makes our knees shake. At least, it should.

Finally, we need to address the question of who should be considered a leader. It could be anyone who has a people following.[7] It could be anyone who aspires to a goal that requires others to participate.[8] Or, as we believe, it could be anyone God has put in spiritual authority over another. Using this definition significantly expands the population of leaders who might benefit from reading this book. This definition, then, includes all hired church staff, any volunteer teachers in the Church, and all parents. This population is large, indeed!

---

5 1 Samuel 16 – 2 Samuel 3

6 Allender, 2006

7 Sample, 2002

8 Maxwell, 1998

If this is the population, can we discern the call that this large body of leaders is to engage in? We believe we can—at least in part. When Jesus gave the Great Commission,[9] He did so to all disciples. He did not exclude anyone, for any reason. Instead, all were given the task to make disciples, wherever they may be found, in whatever situations we may be living in. While we are not saying that all need to be foreign missionaries, we are saying that all followers of Christ are given the spiritual authority and responsibility to make disciples of those in their lives.

Unreasonable? It is God's call on your life if you call Christ your Lord. Impossible? For you alone, yes. With Jesus at your side, not at all. Intimidating? We certainly hope so!

It is with this understanding of leadership within the Church that we are beginning this book. Again, this is intimidating to us; it seems a larger task than our abilities and experience are capable of. This population of leaders is extremely diverse; the population of those they are called to lead is even more diverse. A leadership pattern, then, must take into account this huge diversity and be sensitive to it while still able to sound a clear message for discipleship. This pattern of leadership must call all leaders above themselves and enable them to rise above their leadership limitations. We pray that God has demonstrated that pattern in us as we wrote this book!

Chapter 1 Leadership Reflection:

David's Humble Beginning: Just a Shepherd Boy

> *The LORD said to Samuel, "How long will you grieve over Saul, since I have rejected him from being king over Israel? Fill your horn with oil and go. I will send you to Jesse the Bethlehemite, for I have provided for myself a king among his sons." And Samuel said, "How can I go? If Saul hears it, he will kill me." And the LORD said, "Take a heifer with you and say, 'I have come to sacrifice to the LORD.' And invite Jesse to the sacrifice, and I will show you what you shall do. And you shall anoint for me him whom I declare to you." Samuel did what the LORD commanded and came to Bethlehem. The elders of the city came to meet him trembling and said, "Do you come*

[9] Matthew 28:16–20

peaceably?" And he said, "Peaceably; I have come to sacrifice to the LORD. Consecrate yourselves, and come with me to the sacrifice." And he consecrated Jesse and his sons and invited them to the sacrifice.

When they came, he looked on Eliab and thought, "Surely the LORD's anointed is before him." But the LORD said to Samuel, "Do not look on his appearance or on the height of his stature, because I have rejected him. For the LORD sees not as man sees: man looks on the outward appearance, but the LORD looks on the heart." Then Jesse called Abinadab and made him pass before Samuel. And he said, "Neither has the LORD chosen this one." Then Jesse made Shammah pass by. And he said, "Neither has the LORD chosen this one." And Jesse made seven of his sons pass before Samuel. And Samuel said to Jesse, "The LORD has not chosen these." Then Samuel said to Jesse, "Are all your sons here?" And he said, "There remains yet the youngest, but behold, he is keeping the sheep." And Samuel said to Jesse, "Send and get him, for we will not sit down till he comes here." And he sent and brought him in. Now he was ruddy and had beautiful eyes and was handsome. And the LORD said, "Arise, anoint him, for this is he." Then Samuel took the horn of oil and anointed him in the midst of his brothers. And the Spirit of the LORD rushed upon David from that day forward. And Samuel rose up and went to Ramah. (1 Samuel 16:1–13 ESV)

Personal Reflection:

- Think about David's introduction to kingdom leadership. What would it be like to have been in his shoes?

- Have you faced similar circumstances to David? How has your situation been similar? How has it been different? Jot a few notes if you might find this helpful. (After all David, as a "man after God's own heart," wrote quite a few notes in the Psalms see below!)

David's Journal:

In the passage below, David expresses his heart of praise. Read the passages, preferably aloud, slowly three times to allow David's words to soak in.

O LORD, our Lord, how majestic is your name in all the earth!
You have set your glory above the heavens.
Out of the mouth of babies and infants, you have established strength because of your foes, to still the enemy and the avenger.
When I look at your heavens, the work of your fingers, the moon and the stars, which you have set in place,
what is man that you are mindful of him, and the son of man that you care for him?
Yet you have made him a little lower than the heavenly beings and crowned him with glory and honor.
You have given him dominion over the works of your hands; you have put all things under his feet,
all sheep and oxen, and also the beasts of the field,
the birds of the heavens, and the fish of the sea, whatever passes along the paths of the seas.
O LORD, our Lord, how majestic is your name in all the earth!
(Psalm 8:1–9 ESV)

- What do you sense God sees as He looks in your heart? Lift up your heart of praise before the Lord, as David challenges us to do. Consider writing these words out as David does below.

Further Reflection:

- Recall an important moment in your life when you stepped into the leadership of others. Write down, or list in your mind, the challenges you faced, as well as the appreciation you have for this experience.

- Give God thanks for having served in the leadership capacity He has given you. (One might call this "kingdom leadership," as all things are dedicated to God's glory.)

Chapter 2:

An Understanding of Spiritual Growth

If our call, then, is to make disciples, it would make sense to try to understand the nature of spiritual growth. This is a task that has engaged many great Christian thinkers over the centuries and has been the subject of countless writings. Bruce Demarest reprises many of these writers in his book, *Seasons of the Soul.*[10] In this book, he presents the process of spiritual growth as seasons of orientation and disorientation through which a follower of God must come face to face with struggle, disillusionment, and suffering, in order to fully grasp the union with God that is sought. For this model, he refers to many early Christian writers and mystics who proposed stages of spiritual growth.[11]

It is this concept of stages of spiritual growth that we feel is foundational to the development of any vision of leadership within the church. Failure to grasp the reality of these stages of growth most often results in a vision that is inherently exclusionary to some. Expression and communication of the vision will tend to be in terms of maturity as perceived by the vision creator(s). Those not sharing or grasping the vision are either overtly, or by implication, considered "immature." The nature of this exclusion becomes a hindrance to growth in the Spirit, as one cannot grow faster than God has planned, nor can one grow in a direction contrary to the

[10] Demarest, 2009

[11] In the appendix of his book, Demarest provides a very succinct and clear summary of many of the Christian writers who saw spiritual growth as a stage process.

will of God for the journey of that individual. Any attempts to meet the standard of maturity expressed in the faulty vision will result in a human-empowered growth that will be short-lived at best, or despair-inducing at worst.

> Failure to grasp the reality of these stages of growth most often results in a vision that is inherently exclusionary to some.

An example of this can be seen in visions that present spiritual growth (discipleship) as a baseball diamond.[12] Immature believers start at first base and then progress around the bases of the offered curriculum until they reach home plate. As long as they are not engaging in "home plate" activities or education, they are growing, but they are still immature Christians. Some churches limit roles of participation and/or leadership to those who have completed the maturing process. This creates a "judgment criteria" by which an individual can measure his or her own spiritual maturity or the maturity of others within the flock. Possibly even more challenging (worse) is the idea that a person who has completed the curriculum is a fully mature Christian.

This concept of judgment is actually quite foreign to the New Testament. Even when the writer of Hebrews decries the failure of the church to grow and mature,[13] he is careful not to be very specific about what he is using to make that judgment. In fact, the nature of the issue he is addressing is more that the church is failing to grow, not that it is failing to grow in the way he desired. We will discuss this area in more detail in the next chapter.

> No one person goes through the stages in the exact same way, and no one progresses through the stages in a completely linear way. Instead, it is more accurate to understand the stages as a spiraling cone, each stage revisited many times.

---

[12] Saddleback Church initiated this model that has been widely adopted. We are not addressing Saddleback's specific model, as it has its own unique corrective features. However, the model approach, as implemented by well-meaning churches, has often resulted in the struggles we describe.

[13] Hebrews 5:12ff

With these thoughts in mind, then, we want to walk through the basics of the spiritual growth process we have gained through study of the classical and contemporary Christian writers on the topic. The stages presented are varied and need to be understood as fluid and individual. No one person goes through the stages in the exact same way, and no one progresses through the stages in a completely linear way. Instead, it is more accurate to understand the stages as a spiraling cone, each stage revisited many times as the Holy Spirit guides and challenges the individual with circumstances and growth opportunities.

In his landmark book, *Stages of Faith*, James Fowler[14] addresses what is meant by the term "faith." Here Fowler distinguishes between faith, religion, and belief. He contends that religion is a set of cumulative traditions that define a cultural approach to faith, while belief is the set of data that one has chosen to hold as truth. Faith, on the other hand, is that (or whom) one has set his/her heart on, committed fully to, and dedicated one's loyalty to. Fowler contends that this understanding of faith more closely approximates the New Testament understanding of the word "believe."

In some ways, Fowler's view of faith approaches what we today are terming "worldview." Though Fowler resisted the term in his book, it does represent an understanding of what he is addressing that is more available to people than the very complex understanding that he presents. Using this term and idea, we can understand the development of faith as an integral part of being human. We will develop in faith as we develop our understanding of the world and bring our creativity and logic to bear on what often seems obscure. Our faith will grow in interaction with the surroundings in our lives, including the teachings we are exposed to. Thus, everyone has "faith" as Fowler describes it. We would add that the faith will be more or less valid depending on the degree of truth behind its development. For example, it is possible for a child to develop faith in the tooth fairy and hold a very strong worldview that includes the tooth fairy until such time as that notion is challenged by other children, by parental correction, or by evidence that contradicts the held faith. Children have been known to get involved in physical altercations to defend such a challenged belief.

[14] Fowler, 1981

What we are saying is that revelation from God, from parents, and from society in general forms a crucial part of this faith development. In African tribes where the belief in animism is commonly accepted and unchallenged, the faith development of those tribal members incorporates the belief system surrounding them. In Christian homes, the same can be said; though we would contend that the revelation involved contains a greater degree of actual truth. However, as Christian counselors, we have seen a number of highly distorted views of God coming from strong Christian families. Fowler's approach as a developmentalist is to show how faith develops as an individual grows, no matter the content or validity of that faith.

The point here is that God created humanity to have a relationship with Him. Persons will attempt to function in accordance with that design, regardless of the actual reality behind the worldview presented to them. This is not relativistic, but it is a fact of the human design that God intended. Our understanding would be that a Biblical worldview of "faith" is based on the strong reality of a very specific revelation of God working in history and culminating in the revelation of His Son, Jesus Christ. The basis for knowing this to be truer than other options is not in the scope of this book and can be found in the work of various Christian apologists.

Janet Hagberg and Robert Guelich present a model of spiritual growth in their book, *The Critical Journey*.[15] This six-stage model built on the writings of early Christian thinkers and mystics can be enlightening to our work here. Their work contrasts with that of Fowler in that they are primarily talking about the development of adult faith over an adult lifespan. This approach is more in line with the focus of this book, though Fowler's work can be very meaningful to anyone working to educate children in the Christian faith.

> Our understanding would be that a Biblical worldview of "faith" is based on the strong reality of very specific revelation of God working in history and culminating in the revelation of His Son, Jesus Christ.

[15] Hagberg and Guelich, 2005.

The six stages presented by Hagberg and Guelich are: 1) Recognition of God, 2) Life of Discipleship, 3) Productive Life, 4) Journey Inward and the Wall, 5) Journey Outward, and 6) Life of Love. Each stage is characterized by distinct understandings of God and our relationship with Him and our actions in response to that understanding. The authors are careful to caution against seeing the stages as absolute or sequential, stating that the stages may be revisited, and one may be in more than one stage at a time. Yet, consistent with stage theories, each represents distinct and measurable changes in thinking and action with some degree of predictable sequencing.

Stage 1, Recognition of God, is a time of coming to the realization that God is big, and we are essentially powerless over some very important things in our lives. Our image of God is uninformed and vague; He is just powerful and gracious. Awareness of the miraculous is strong, and God's love for us is overwhelming.

We add to the work of Hagberg and Guelich from our work with relationships and people. This helps us see a commonality with the development of all interpersonal relationships. Based on our work as counselors, we could characterize this first stage as the idealization stage of any relationship. In this stage, God, or the idealized other, is perfect, without blemish, and fully meets our expectations. We are reminded of the enthusiastic gushing of a friend describing early dates with a newly found loved one. What is of significance here is that the impressions are often not completely based in reality but are projected onto the other by one's own expectations and longings. This is also true of this stage with God. The God we see in this stage is a mixture of truth and our projections. We tend to see things that validate our projections and overlook things that challenge them.

Stage 1 gives way to Stage 2, the Life of Discipleship. In this stage is a realization that we do not know all there is to know about God and His expectations of us. We then seek to learn and align ourselves to a greater degree than we did before. We understand that we do not live for ourselves alone.

Again, this stage correlates well to relationship dynamics. As we move from our initial euphoria over meeting our perfect mate, we begin to attempt to learn as much as we can about them, their favorite color, food, styles, books, movies, etc. We seek to modify our behavior to be more pleasing to them based on what we learn about their preferences. In this stage, new or renewed believers will seek to learn all they can about God and His desires for their lives. This stage sees a strong sense of right versus wrong and a tendency to judge maturity on the basis of right thinking and right actions.

Stage 3, the Life of Productivity, is characterized by outward actions and service. In this stage, the individual seeks to put the knowledge gained in Stage 2 into practice for the good of the community and the world. This stage sees people doing the right things for mixed reasons. A strong sense of expected outcomes is a part of this stage. God's blessing on our efforts is seen by the achievement of the expected outcomes.

In other interpersonal relationships, we see this as the stage of life together. There are explicit and implicit agreements on work sharing, roles, and duties. For example, as long as the husband goes to work and brings home his income and engages in family life and the emotional needs of his wife, all is good. The wife also meets her expected roles as a mother, possibly as a partner in wage earning, and as a supporter of the emotional needs of her husband. This stage can be as prolonged for as long as the equilibrium of balanced expectations can be maintained.

Stage 4, the Wall, is a difficult stage. This stage is a time of disequilibration, stress, and unmet expectations. Persons at this stage become aware of a deeper dissatisfaction with the status quo and a greater awareness of expectations that are not being met. This can occur as a result of a change in circumstances that has unacceptable consequences in the mind of the individual, or it can occur as one realizes that expectations that were delayed may not ever be met.

Relationally, we see couples in this stage when children are now off to school and the delayed desires for deeper connections move from delayed to current. We also see it as individuals reach the "empty nest" phase of life and look for things in each other that children and previously career satisfied. With God, this is a time of questioning. Does God really care? Are the things I have believed in ever going to happen? Is my faith based on anything real, or is it all simply my own fantastical projections? John of the Cross called this "the dark night of the soul," and it is truly dark as it challenges the core of what we have believed to be meaningful. Unsuccessful resolution of this stage leads to despondency and despair.

Successful resolution of Stage 4 moves us to Stage 5, the Journey Outward. This movement is a function of an increased ability to surrender to God. It involves allowing God to have His way with us, regardless of our desires or expectations. Individuals in Stage 5 are more like Job, when he reached the point in his dialogue with God in the storm when he stated, "I am unworthy—how can I reply to you? I put my hand over my mouth. I spoke once, but I have no answer—twice, but I will say no more."[16] We come to realize that God is infinitely wiser than we are, and that His will and way are acceptable, even if it brings us pain in the moment.

At many levels, this is a matured return to Stage 1, in that we again see our powerlessness and God's awe-inspiring power. It is matured in that we now see better how God has chosen to use us in His work, but not according to our expectations. We are willing to be used in His way without demands of our own.

Finally, Stage 6, the Life of Love, is reached when all efforts to accomplish anything measurable by our world's standards are abandoned, and we live simply as a reflection of God's love in whatever circumstances He places us in. This stage is rare, and often we live it only in glimpses. To those not in this stage, anyone living in it can seem aimless and unmotivated. This stage is where we live out the journey as the destination in ways beyond mere cliché.

We will use the basic foundations of Hagberg and Guelich's[17] work as a guide to the remainder of this book. Mixed in will be the understandings of Fowler, Kohlberg, Demarest, and others, as well as our experience as leaders and counselors. Seeing the task of leadership with a grasp of these stages will benefit our ability to expand our leadership of those God has placed in our lives. Each stage represents leadership challenges and opportunities. The

[16] Job 40:4–5

[17] Hagberg and Guelich, 2005

temptation is to lead those who are near our current stage. This is familiar and comfortable, but it is not what God has called the Church to be.

Chapter 2 Leadership Reflection:

David Expresses God's Own Heart: Sparing Saul's Life

> *When Saul returned from following the Philistines, he was told, "Behold, David is in the wilderness of Engedi." Then Saul took three thousand chosen men out of all Israel and went to seek David and his men in front of the Wildgoats' Rocks. And he came to the sheepfolds by the way, where there was a cave, and Saul went in to relieve himself. Now David and his men were sitting in the innermost parts of the cave. And the men of David said to him, "Here is the day of which the LORD said to you, 'Behold, I will give your enemy into your hand, and you shall do to him as it shall seem good to you.' "Then David arose and stealthily cut off a corner of Saul's robe. And afterward David's heart struck him, because he had cut off a corner of Saul's robe. He said to his men, "The LORD forbid that I should do this thing to my LORD, the LORD's anointed, to put out my hand against him, seeing he is the LORD's anointed." So David persuaded his men with these words and did not permit them to attack Saul. And Saul rose up and left the cave and went on his way.* (1 Samuel 24 1–7 ESV)

Personal Reflection:

- David was standing against the current when he spared Saul's life. His walk of faith with the Lord led him in a direction his men would not choose. In leadership, one might face this dilemma often. How have you seen God go before you in these cases? Have there been times where His Presence was not clear?

- Leadership teams can have members at various stages of faith, as mentioned in this chapter. How might this influence the leadership of those you serve?

Further Reflection:

- Recall an instance where the stand you took was not with the majority. Preferably, jot down or list in your mind the challenge you faced in this, as well as the appreciation you have for this experience.

David's Journal:

Read the following Psalm, preferably aloud. For even deeper meaning, read the passage slowly three times as follows:

The LORD is my light and my salvation; whom shall I fear?
The LORD is the stronghold of my life; of whom shall I be afraid?

When evildoers assail me to eat up my flesh,
my adversaries and foes, it is they who stumble and fall.

Though an army encamp against me, my heart shall not fear;
though war arise against me, yet I will be confident.

One thing have I asked of the LORD, that will I seek after:
that I may dwell in the house of the LORD all the days of my life,
to gaze upon the beauty of the LORD and to inquire in his temple.

For he will hide me in his shelter in the day of trouble;
he will conceal me under the cover of his tent; he will lift me high upon a rock.

And now my head shall be lifted up above my enemies all around me, and I will offer in his tent sacrifices with shouts of joy;
I will sing and make melody to the LORD.

Hear, O LORD, when I cry aloud; be gracious to me and answer me!
You have said, "Seek my face."
My heart says to you, "Your face, LORD, do I seek." Hide not your face from me.
Turn not your servant away in anger, O you who have been my help. Cast me not off; forsake me not, O God of my salvation!
For my father and my mother have forsaken me, but the LORD will take me in.

Teach me your way, O LORD, and lead me on a level path because of my enemies.
Give me not up to the will of my adversaries; for false witnesses have risen against me, and they breathe out violence.

I believe that I shall look upon the goodness of the LORD in the land of the living!
Wait for the LORD; be strong, and let your heart take courage; wait for the LORD!
(Psalm 27:1–14 ESV)

Personal Reflection:

- What is God teaching you about being a leader through the readings?

- What is God sharing with you about His leadership through His words?

Chapter 3:

The Leader's Stages of Faith

Having a basic understanding of the growth of faith and the patterns it may follow, inevitably leads to self-evaluation. In the case of the leader, this can create some degree of angst. Leaders, by definition (at least in this world), are supposed to know more and be more advanced in preparation for whatever task or assignment they are to lead than those they are leading. This problem stems from the faulty understanding that the later stages of faith are more advanced than the earlier stages. The numbering of stages and using such terms as "maturing" or even "growth" are deceptive when applied to these stages.

When I (Michael) fell in love with Valerie, I certainly engaged our relationship at the idealization stage. I can remember telling my friends and family of all the wonderful qualities and attributes that this newfound person possessed. My enthusiasm was great, and all that I perceived was at least mostly true. Now, thirty-some years later, my love for Valerie has changed. My tendency is to use the words "grown" and "matured," or that I love her more now than then. However, that does a great disservice to the love of those early years. Were you to ask me whether I love her more now than then, I would be hard-pressed to say yes. My love has changed, but I would hesitate to say it is stronger. The changes are immense, and we struggle to find language to encapsulate the nature of these changes. More often than not, we settle for growth. My most recent visit to the greeting-card counter gave strong evidence of this struggle. In a culture where so much of everything is comparative, the application of comparative expressions to describe changes is rampant. My love today is not better or worse than my love in those earlier years; it is not stronger or weaker; it is not more or less. It is simply different. And, if it were not different, I would suspect that it was stuck in place.

Change is the nature of any relationship, and no change implies a lack of health.

Change is the nature of any relationship, and no change implies a lack of health. We have told many married or soon-to-be married couples that their relationships are either growing or dying. While this conveys the appropriate message to always be at work on a relationship, it also conveys the false impression that the next phases are better than the one the couple is now in.

These inappropriate ideas about the comparative nature of relationships need to be corrected for spiritual leadership to be effective. While the leader may be at the third stage of faith, leadership of those in the other stages is not precluded. This is why understanding the stages as a spiraling cone[18] is important. The leaders who understand the nature of this know that wherever they are, they are both ahead of and behind all other stages. The insights of each stage have something to say to the other stages, and the primary characteristics of each stage serve as a corrective lens to those in other stages. Thus, the very nature of the development of relationships offers a mutuality to all believers in all stages, whether leaders or otherwise.

There are also some inherent blind spots for leaders in whichever stage they may be. These blind spots can be minimized or eliminated altogether if the leaders can do honest self-assessments and possesses sufficient humility to address them. These blind spots will be covered in detail in the chapters dealing with each stage, but they are addressed here to help leaders to focus on the importance of the task of knowing where they are on the relational journey with God.

[18] Demarest, 2009

Insightful leaders, though, will look for and take advantage of the strengths of each stage as they learn to perceive them in others.

The most significant and visible blind spot of leading without knowledge of the stages of faith is revealed when leaders project their stages on everyone. When this occurs, leaders who are in the growth stage believe that everyone is as hungry as they are for information and seek to force those in their circle of influence into a learning environment. Leaders in the "sharing of faith" stage with this blind spot will seek to force everyone into productive programs they have set up. Leaders who are living out the call with this blind spot will fail to set up educational or productive opportunities for others, as they assume that all know and will respond to God's call in their lives.

Insightful leaders, though, will look for and take advantage of the strengths of each stage as they learn to perceive them in others. They will also know that individuals should not be pigeonholed into roles that preclude further movement in the stages of faith development. Instead, they will be looking for opportunities to assist them, and themselves, in moving into the next stages.

Chapter 3 Leadership Reflection:

David Changes His Plans

> *Now Samuel died. And all Israel assembled and mourned for him, and they buried him in his house at Ramah. Then David rose and went down to the wilderness of Paran. And there was a man in Maon whose business was in Carmel. The man was very rich; he had three thousand sheep and a thousand goats. He was shearing his sheep in Carmel. Now the name of the man was Nabal, and the name of his wife Abigail. The woman was discerning and beautiful, but the man was harsh and badly behaved; he was a Calebite. David heard in the wilderness that Nabal was shearing his sheep. So David sent ten young men. And David said to the young men, "Go up to Carmel, and go to Nabal and greet him in my name. And thus you shall greet him: 'Peace be to you, and peace be to your house, and peace be to all that you have. I hear that you have shearers. Now*

your shepherds have been with us, and we did them no harm, and they missed nothing all the time they were in Carmel. Ask your young men, and they will tell you. Therefore let my young men find favor in your eyes, for we come on a feast day. Please give whatever you have at hand to your servants and to your son David.'"

When David's young men came, they said all this to Nabal in the name of David, and then they waited. And Nabal answered David's servants, "Who is David? Who is the son of Jesse? There are many servants these days who are breaking away from their masters. Shall I take my bread and my water and my meat that I have killed for my shearers and give it to men who come from I do not know where?" So David's young men turned away and came back and told him all this. And David said to his men, "Every man strap on his sword!" And every man of them strapped on his sword. David also strapped on his sword. And about four hundred men went up after David, while two hundred remained with the baggage.

But one of the young men told Abigail, Nabal's wife, "Behold, David sent messengers out of the wilderness to greet our master, and he railed at them. Yet the men were very good to us, and we suffered no harm, and we did not miss anything when we were in the fields, as long as we went with them. They were a wall to us both by night and by day, all the while we were with them keeping the sheep. Now therefore know this and consider what you should do, for harm is determined against our master and against all his house, and he is such a worthless man that one cannot speak to him."

Then Abigail made haste and took two hundred loaves and two skins of wine and five sheep already prepared and five seahs of parched grain and a hundred clusters of raisins and two hundred cakes of figs, and laid them on donkeys. And she said to her young men, "Go on before me; behold, I come after you." But she did not tell her husband Nabal. And as she rode on the donkey and came down under cover of the mountain, behold, David and his men came down toward her, and she met them. Now David had said, "Surely in vain have I guarded all that this fellow has in the wilderness, so that nothing was missed of all that belonged to him, and he has returned me evil for good. God do so to the enemies of David and more also, if by morning I leave so much as one male of all who belong to him."

When Abigail saw David, she hurried and got down from the donkey and fell before David on her face and bowed to the ground. She fell at his feet and said, "On me alone, my LORD, be the guilt. Please let your servant speak in your ears, and hear the words of your servant. Let not my LORD regard this worthless fellow, Nabal, for as his name is, so is he. Nabal is his name, and folly is with him. But I your servant did not see the young men of my LORD, whom you sent. Now then, my LORD, as the LORD lives, and as your soul lives, because the LORD has restrained you from bloodguilt and from saving with your own hand, now then let your enemies and those who seek to do evil to my LORD be as Nabal. And now let this present that your servant has brought to my LORD be given to the young men who follow my LORD. Please forgive the trespass of your servant. For the LORD will certainly make my LORD a sure house, because my LORD is fighting the battles of the LORD, and evil shall not be found in you so long as you live. If men rise up to pursue you and to seek your life, the life of my LORD shall be bound in the bundle of the living in the care of the LORD your God. And the lives of your enemies he shall sling out as from the hollow of a sling. And when the LORD has done to my LORD according to all the good that he has spoken concerning you and has appointed you prince over Israel, my LORD shall have no cause of grief or pangs of conscience for having shed blood without cause or for my LORD taking vengeance himself. And when the LORD has dealt well with my LORD, then remember your servant."

And David said to Abigail, "Blessed be the LORD, the God of Israel, who sent you this day to meet me! Blessed be your discretion, and blessed be you, who have kept me this day from bloodguilt and from avenging myself with my own hand! For as surely as the LORD, the God of Israel, lives, who has restrained me from hurting you, unless you had hurried and come to meet me, truly by morning there had not been left to Nabal so much as one male." Then David received from her hand what she had brought him. And he said to her, "Go up in peace to your house. See, I have obeyed your voice, and I have granted your petition."

When Abigail went to Nabal, he was in the house holding a banquet like that of a king. He was in high spirits and very drunk. So she told him nothing at all until daybreak. Then in the morning, when Nabal was sober, his wife told him all these things, and his heart failed him and he became like a stone. About ten days later, the LORD struck Nabal and he died.

When David heard that Nabal was dead, he said, "Praise be to the LORD, who has upheld my cause against Nabal for treating me with contempt. He has kept his servant from doing wrong and has brought Nabal's wrongdoing down on his own head."

Then David sent word to Abigail, asking her to become his wife. His servants went to Carmel and said to Abigail, "David has sent us to you to take you to become his wife."

She bowed down with her face to the ground and said, "I am your servant and am ready to serve you and wash the feet of my LORD's servants." Abigail quickly got on a donkey and, attended by her five female servants, went with David's messengers and became his wife. David had also married Ahinoam of Jezreel, and they both were his wives. But Saul had given his daughter Michal, David's wife, to Paltiel son of Laish, who was from Gallim. (1 Samuel 25:1–44 ESV)

Personal Reflection:

- What was David's response to Abigail? How did he adjust his plans as he saw her discretion and faith?

- Has there been an instance where God called you to adjust your plans in response to a faithful brother or sister? How did it work out?

Jesus Adjusts His Focus to Those Expressing Need

Then they came to Jericho. As Jesus and his disciples, together with a large crowd, were leaving the city, a blind man, Bartimaeus (which means "son of Timaeus"), was sitting by the roadside begging. When he heard that it was Jesus of Nazareth, he began to shout, "Jesus, Son of David, have mercy on me!"

Many rebuked him and told him to be quiet, but he shouted all the more, "Son of David, have mercy on me!"

Jesus stopped and said, "Call him."

So they called to the blind man, "Cheer up! On your feet! He's calling you." Throwing his cloak aside, he jumped to his feet and came to Jesus.

"What do you want me to do for you?" Jesus asked him.

The blind man said, "Rabbi, I want to see."

"Go," said Jesus, "your faith has healed you." Immediately he received his sight and followed Jesus along the road. (Mark 10:46–52 NIV)

Personal Reflection:

- Leadership of others at various stages of faith, like David and like Jesus Himself, may call for adjustment on your part, as God leads you. In honesty, is this something you are willing to consider? Jot down some thoughts about this: when would this be difficult and when might it be easy?

- Who might be in your midst who can help you see and meet these types of needs? How might you empower them?

David's Journal:

Read these passages out loud slowly three times. Journal your thoughts.

- 1st READING: Focus on the overall message of these passages.
- 2nd READING: Note the verses that stand out to you during this reading.
- 3rd READING: Consider what deepened understanding, call to action, or invitation to further discernment is inspired in you.

I will give thanks to the LORD with my whole heart; I will recount all of your wonderful deeds.
I will be glad and exult in you; I will sing praise to your name, O Most High.

When my enemies turn back, they stumble and perish before your presence.
For you have maintained my just cause; you have sat on the throne, giving righteous judgment.

You have rebuked the nations; you have made the wicked perish; you have blotted out their name forever and ever.
The enemy came to an end in everlasting ruins; their cities you rooted out; the very memory of them has perished.

But the LORD sits enthroned forever; he has established his throne for justice,
and he judges the world with righteousness; he judges the peoples with uprightness.

The LORD is a stronghold for the oppressed, a stronghold in times of trouble.
And those who know your name put their trust in you, for you, O LORD, have not forsaken those who seek you.

Sing praises to the LORD, who sits enthroned in Zion! Tell among the peoples his deeds!
For he who avenges blood is mindful of them; he does not forget the cry of the afflicted.

Be gracious to me, O Lord! See my affliction from those who hate me, O you who lift me up from the gates of death,
that I may recount all your praises, that in the gates of the daughter of Zion I may rejoice in your salvation.

The nations have sunk in the pit that they made; in the net that they hid, their own foot has been caught.
The Lord has made himself known; he has executed judgment; the wicked are snared in the work of their own hands. Higgaion. Selah

The wicked shall return to Sheol, all the nations that forget God.

For the needy shall not always be forgotten, and the hope of the poor shall not perish forever.

Arise, O Lord! Let not man prevail; let the nations be judged before you! Put them in fear, O Lord! Let the nations know that they are but men! Selah (Psalm 9:1–20 ESV)

Further Reflection:

Note the passion that David had in his relationships with others, his praise and confidence in the Lord, and his concern for his and others' affliction.

- What stirs your passion towards others? Has this ever been challenging?

- What do you appreciate about your heart toward yourself and others?

If you are willing, take this opportunity to share this heart with the Lord, either by journaling to God or in conversation with Him.

Chapter 4:

The Beginning of Faith

Before we begin discussing the particulars of each stage of faith and what it might mean to a leader, we should probably discuss the value of analysis. For this discussion, we borrow from the work of Thomas H. Green, where he writes of those who object to the analysis of their stage of faith as being "too introspective."[19] He acknowledges the validity of the objection, noting that there exists a fine line between analysis and introspection. He goes on and introduces the idea of using this analysis as a map, to be used in direction setting and way finding, if you will, but not to be overly studied and concentrated on.

This is a useful understanding for the leader seeking to set a course for a church or even a single individual. A map has a starting point and desired waypoints along a journey. We have spent much time traveling about the United States. It has always been helpful to consult a map before we begin our road trip, check on our progress periodically, and know when we have arrived at our stopping points. This became especially true as we started traveling in our 36-foot RV, pulling a truck behind us. The consequences of a wrong turn and the ability to turn around became increasingly complex.

So it is with our spiritual journeys. We need to know the starting point, the waypoints, and the direction of the endpoint (though we never reach that in this life). As we progress along the way,

[19] Green, 2007

the complexity increases and we gain baggage (both needed and unneeded), making redirection more and more difficult. Nonetheless, it is important to use the map and make corrections, or we may become hopeless wanderers, making no real progress.

Each stage of the spiritual journey needs to be fully experienced, too. Again, it is the journey that is important, not so much the destination, as cliché as that sounds. It would be totally inappropriate for a leader to recognize the stage an individual is in and to rush to help that person reach the next stage. Yes, set the direction, provide some guidance, but let the experience of the journey and the rate of movement be set by the working of the Holy Spirit in that individual. To do otherwise would be like traveling from one place to another and seeing nothing of the beauty of the land between the destinations.

With this in mind, we return to the first stage, the beginning of faith. In this stage, one becomes aware of God and His characteristic or characteristics that the individual seems to need most. This stage would best correspond to what Fowler called the mythic-literal.[20] Here the individual is grasping the stories of God (including non-biblical stories) without a great deal of discernment. In fact, discernment is a product of the next stage, and too much of it should not be expected here.

It is this starting place the leader needs to understand or else much damage can be done. When a mother has lost her child to death, she is not interested in the omniscience of God, but in His mercy and compassion. If she is just becoming aware of God in this circumstance, she will feel the unexplainable reassurance that God's compassion gives her. She will focus on the loss Jesus' mother, Mary, must have faced. She will find comfort in the fact that God, the Father, felt the loss of His son as deeply as she feels the loss of her child.

It would be both wrong and inconsiderate to try to take this woman and force her into a setting where she is confronted with the righteous judgment of God, or even a setting where she is challenged to learn about all the many attributes of God. That time will come, but not in this first stage. Instead, the leader who is leading beyond his or her own limits will seek to surround this woman with the

[20] Fowler, 1981

loving and gentle characteristics of God, finding them embodied in the Church, the true Body of Christ on this earth. The leader will help to connect her with people who can and will embrace her pain with understanding and compassion and who will allow her to express her confusion and searching without criticalness.

God hears the need and presents Himself as the true answer to the issue. The leader will listen to the story of what God is doing in the life of the one seeking guidance and look for an opportunity to build on it.

There are many such starting points God uses to draw people to Him. It may be recognition of sin, an addiction, or an overwhelming burden of guilt about a committed wrong. It may be the rescue from an oppressive burden of debt, physical pain, or illness of a loved one. It may simply be the need of rescue from one or more of these issues. We cannot anticipate them all, but we can be sure that God can and does. He hears the need and presents Himself as the true answer to the issue. The leader will listen to the story of what God is doing in the life of the one seeking guidance and look for an opportunity to build on it.

An example of this stage can be found in the calling of Peter by Jesus.[21] After a long night of fruitless fishing, Jesus miraculously fills the nets of Simon Peter, meeting his need. Peter's reaction is characteristic of this stage when he exclaims, "Depart from me, for I am a sinful man, O Lord!" Peter's encounter with God in the flesh met one need and revealed an even greater need.

Another time, we see the disciples at sea in a storm, fearful for their lives.[22] After they awaken Jesus, and He demonstrates His power over even the elemental forces of nature, they marvel in awe at who this person is. This awe is another characteristic of this stage. It is important to note that even as Jesus spent time with the disciples, He allowed them to misunderstand His role, knowing that understanding would come in time. He did not agree with their misconceptions, and He absolutely told them only the truth about

[21] Luke 5:1–8

[22] Matthew 8:23–27

Himself, but He did not force into their brokenness and insist on healing that was for a later stage.

One of the features of those in this stage, is a focus on the miraculous. This is especially true of those who are in need of rescue from some aspect of worldly concerns. They see the promises God has made for worldly peace, prosperity, and health and latch onto them like a drowning man latches onto his lifesaver. They see God as this lifesaver, and part of drawing to Him is the application of these promises to their area of need. We have seen leaders who seemed to feel that their task was to lower the expectations of such belief. In fact, we listened to a sermon, a week following a testimonial from a woman who had been cured of her cancer. This leader, fearful that others who had not been healed may fall into depression or despair, preached a sermon on the capricious nature of God's sovereignty. This kind of misrepresentation of God does its own damage, not only to those in this stage, but to those in all stages of faith.

While it is true that God does not heal everyone, or rescue everyone from their worldly oppressions, He is present and caring in each and every situation. It does not hurt to allow faith at this stage to look for and anticipate the miraculous. We have seen it occur often enough to know that God uses these miracles to accomplish His will in His own timing. What is needed at this stage is to help the individual to see the goodness of God in the aspects that have been made attractive to them in their circumstances.

A leader of those in this stage of faith will seek to validate the experience of God that is occurring in their lives and arrange opportunities to celebrate and share these experiences. These opportunities need not be testimonials before the church, though that is not precluded. There are many venues for sharing, and if the leader is encouraging that sharing, the individual often has a greater variety of options than the leader might.

This is an exciting stage, so full of wonder and awareness of the greatness of God. We have seen many in this stage of faith over our years of ministry. We saw hundreds in this stage as we introduced

God to those He led us to in Russia (shortly after the doors opened). In those three years, the curiosity was great and the experience of God in a very challenging time was strong. Later, in our church ministry setting, we saw many new believers in this stage over the years (some years we saw 30% of the church in it). As the apostle Paul told the Thessalonians, "Do not quench the Spirit."[23] It is a time to celebrate, a time to embrace the experience, and a time to rejoice!

To be sure, individuals in this stage of faith often interpret their experience of God through their own brokenness and need. That does not invalidate their experience, but it points to the need for the leader to facilitate venues for movement toward healing of that brokenness. If the brokenness that God is using to woo this individual to Himself is grief, then a grief support group might be warranted. If the need is financial, some physical support along with budgeting classes can be provided. If the need is addiction, recovery groups become an option. When the need is marital challenges, marriage counseling or mentoring can be set up.

This list goes on, and we need to emphasize that as healing begins, so the journey toward the next stage begins. It is also key that the leader determines that each group can celebrate how God is working in the life of the individual. Groups that do not do this or are hostile toward the idea of their experience with God are counterproductive to growth of this stage.

Finally, looking to the next stage, the leader wants to encourage the growing and developing hunger to know more about this good God who is being experienced. It is natural that an individual in this stage starts to desire to know more about the Person who has ignited such joy in them. This is not an activity, but an imbedded attitude that celebrates and communicates, "If you think this is cool, just wait! You ain't seen nothing yet!"

[23] 1 Thessalonians 5:19

Chapter 4 Leadership Reflection:

Come Follow Me! The Calling of the First Disciples

> *On one occasion, while the crowd was pressing in on him to hear the word of God, he was standing by the lake of Gennesaret, and he saw two boats by the lake, but the fishermen had gone out of them and were washing their nets. Getting into one of the boats, which was Simon's, he asked him to put out a little from the land. And he sat down and taught the people from the boat. And when he had finished speaking, he said to Simon, "Put out into the deep and let down your nets for a catch."*
>
> *And Simon answered, "Master, we toiled all night and took nothing! But at your word I will let down the nets." And when they had done this, they enclosed a large number of fish, and their nets were breaking. They signaled to their partners in the other boat to come and help them. And they came and filled both the boats, so that they began to sink. But when Simon Peter saw it, he fell down at Jesus' knees, saying, "Depart from me, for I am a sinful man, O Lord." For he and all who were with him were astonished at the catch of fish that they had taken, and so also were James and John, sons of Zebedee, who were partners with Simon.*
>
> *And Jesus said to Simon, "Do not be afraid; from now on you will be catching men." And when they had brought their boats to land, they left everything and followed him.* (Luke 5:1–11 ESV)

Personal Reflection:

- Is there a time early in your leadership (or in the life of a leader you know) when you took a leap of faith, went for the seemingly impossible, like Peter, and "Put out into the deep and let down your nets for a catch," and amazing things happened? Briefly write about this was experienced.

- In this seemingly impossible situation, was there any sense of being deserving or undeserving? What was your response and the responses of those around you after this "miracle" took place?

- How might you encourage first stagers as they approach or share their leaps of faith in following Jesus?

Further Reflection:

Step Out onto Holy Ground! The Calling of Moses

Read these passages out loud slowly three times. Journal your thoughts.

- 1st READING: Focus on the overall message of these passages.
- 2nd READING: Note the verses that stand out to you during this reading.
- 3rd READING: Consider what deepened understanding, call to action, or invitation to further discernment is inspired in you.

Now Moses was keeping the flock of his father-in-law, Jethro, the priest of Midian, and he led his flock to the west side of the wilderness and came to Horeb, the mountain of God. And the angel of the Lord *appeared to him in a flame of fire out of the midst of a bush. He looked, and behold, the bush was burning, yet it was not consumed. And Moses said, "I will turn aside to see this great sight, why the bush is not burned." When the* Lord *saw that he turned aside to see, God called to him out of the bush, "Moses, Moses!" And he said, "Here I am." Then he said, "Do not come near; take your sandals off your feet, for the place on which you are standing is holy ground." And he said, "I am the God of your father, the God of Abraham, the God of Isaac, and the God of Jacob." And Moses hid his face, for he was afraid to look at God. (Exodus 3:1–6* ESV*)*

- Have there been times in your leadership journey when seeing the miracle before you was more challenging than encouraging?

- Like Moses, are you called to greater leadership, yet there is a sense of unworthiness or timidity that holds you back?

- How might those you serve be built up as they wrestle with beginning their leadership journey of faith?

Chapter 5: The Growth of Faith

We once knew a man who had met Jesus and experienced the first stage of the faith journey. His experience of Jesus was miraculous, and this man was full of joy and expectation. He wanted to share that joy with everyone he knew, and he set about doing just that. However, he soon encountered some difficulties in describing who this Person was that he was attempting to share. He could very effectively share the experience, but he found he was lacking in knowledge about the Person involved in the experience. This man's response was to set about educating himself about God in a very systematic way. He obtained a variety of Bible translations, commentaries, historical commentaries, works of various apologists, and even language assistance resources for the Greek and Hebrew of the Bible. He was often found buried behind these stacks of books for hours at a time as he sought to gain an understanding of just who God is. He signed up for any class that he could that would give him more information about both God and how to share about God.

While this response is more on the extreme end of the stage we have called "the growth of faith," it well illustrates the movement from Stage 1 to Stage 2 of faith development. This second stage seeks to move beyond the experience and supplement that experience with knowledge. As we noted earlier, in any relationship, the enthusiastic shine moves to a time of information gathering. At least a part of this is driven by a desire to return pleasure to the One who is giving pleasure. And, in order to know what gives pleasure, one must learn about the likes and dislikes, about the things that draw and the things that repel, even the things that are more neutral.

> This second stage seeks to move beyond the experience and supplement that experience with knowledge.

The leader who is sensitive to these stages of faith and seeks to encourage and honor them will see to it that the individual is given the opportunity to gain this knowledge in accordance with that person's interests and abilities. This leader will also try to discern the motive behind such information gathering efforts as that may indicate a direction to point.

An example of this might be the efforts of a young man who immersed himself in studies surrounding the sovereignty of God. He studied all of the Reformation writings, searched out the Bible passages, and asked many questions of anyone who would engage with him. When his motive for such study was sought, he revealed a deep fear that this good God that he had come to love might be capable of abandoning him, of "not choosing" him. It was important to direct his efforts more toward an understanding of the loving and fully accepting nature of God to those who accepted and believed upon His Son. When he was able to grasp the full assurance of God and that those who place themselves under the redeeming blood of Jesus Christ were indeed saved, he was able to move on to learn about other aspects of God's nature. The unfortunate part of this story is that the leader (myself, Michael) was slow to seek this motive, and the young man spent many unnecessary months in an unreasonable fear of losing (or never really having) his salvation.

It is our opinion, based on our experience, that the best and most profitable question to answer in the early part of this stage of faith revolves around the goodness of God. Is God really (always) good, and if so, can I trust that goodness to be poured out upon me? When this question is answered in the positive and is fully grasped and understood, other aspects of God's nature in which His goodness is sometimes more difficult to see are kept in perspective. This is a foundation of faith that is not easily shaken in later stages.

The goodness of God is best seen to the eyes of a broken humanity in the gift of the Son. Understanding the cost to God (to the whole of the Trinity) of that gift early in the faith walk is so helpful to facing some of the struggles that arrive in later stages. Anything a leader can do to provide this teaching and to help anchor it deeply in the soul of the individual in this stage is not to be treated as a lesser priority.

> **The best and most profitable question to answer in the early part of this stage of faith revolves around the goodness of God.**

This is also a time to introduce the concept of mystery, of a God greater than our mind's capacity to grasp. Reducing God to what our minds can fathom makes a god of our creation rather than of God's creation. The concept of mystery, of being able to conceive of a God whose "thoughts are higher than ours"[24] is one that sets a boundary around what we can and cannot know about God and His ways. It helps us avoid the chasing of "irreverent babble" and "foolish controversies"[25] and keeps one on the focus of what is faith-building.

Conversely, a focus on inappropriate things can lead to a weak foundation of faith. A faith that is founded on the question of whether I will escape hell is such a weak foundation. This is not to say that we should not desire to escape hell; nor should the eternal separation from God be treated lightly. Jesus did not avoid it altogether, and neither should we. However, our point is that a faith that is founded upon escaping from hell does not see the true nature of God well. It often is little more than the escape from an angry and unpredictable poor parent. When presented with challenge, this faith often evaporates like a mist.

Another egregious example of widespread error is found in churches who make their particular focus and approach (their vision and values) the point of entry for the educational aspect of their ministry. While this makes a lot of sense from an institutional loyalty point of view, and has a place in the next stage of faith, it does little to help the believer see their place as a part of a whole Body of Christ. Instead, it locates the Body within the structure of that particular church and its expression of the work of the church. It builds loyalty to a single church or denomination on the basis of institutional values over a greater membership in the whole of the Body of Christ. By nature, it declares that this church is doing a better job and joining the church

24 Isaiah 55:9

25 1 Timothy 6:20; Titus 3:9

in this is more right than other ways or expressions. In the long run, this approach can damage faith, as an individual encounters the brokenness that is bound to be revealed within the walls of any church. There is little foundation to fall back on when they inevitably see the leadership and/or membership exposed as sinful parts of the broken humanity to which we all belong. The foundation has been built on a manmade vision rather than on the loving goodness of God.

Throughout this stage, a maturing growth is occurring that moves beyond the foundation of the goodness and mystery of God. As this maturing develops, the leader will need to be watchful that it remains motivated rightly. There are many who know much about God, but who are never able to personalize it into a relational understanding. Guiding all learning about God toward this understanding of its relational purpose grows the indwelling Upper Room of our souls[26] and engages that mysterious working of the Holy Spirit.

Certainly, the church has a long history of education for this stage of faith. The catechisms of the Reformers are just such an effort. Even before that, in a time of illiteracy and general lack of education, the use of imagery was prevalent to teach and preserve essential truths about God and His nature. We encountered an example of this in Russia when we had the opportunity to teach there shortly after the Curtain came down in the early 1990s. We encountered a great hunger for the message we carried, and as we began teaching classes, we found a surprising underlying basic knowledge of the general storyline of the Bible and its major themes. After all, the Soviet government did everything it could to suppress religion and its teachings for a 70-year period. As we inquired about how they knew these basic stories, we were told the museums contained the great works of art from Christian times and the stories associated with these had been taught to them as myths. In addition, the Russian Orthodox churches that had been allowed to remain were full of detailed images that many could recite the meaning of.

In our more modern eras, we see Christian universities and seminaries dedicated to training church leadership in this key area of

[26] Crabb, *Safest Place on Earth: Where people Connect and Are Forever Changed,* 1999

growth. We ourselves are products of some of these, and we celebrate what we received from them. In many ways, the world of today is more prepared and able to meet the needs of this stage of faith than in any other era of history. Today, we have instant access to so much information via the internet, we have well-trained theologians leading our churches, and we have trained educational specialists to develop curriculum and distribution systems designed to make sure it is widely available. We have never in history had an opportunity to have the level of information about the nature of God so readily available.

Yet, this is itself part of a new problem facing the leader. It is no longer sufficient to simply provide the materials one thinks are best. The leader of today's church must be aware of much of the material that is available and be able to help the eager learner rightly discern what it worth pursuing and what is not. Just as Jesus said of the wheat and the tares,[27] the materials available today are over-sown with the weeds of the enemy, and help is needed to navigate the muddied waters. The leader should no longer seek to be the most knowledgeable or the most charismatic in presentation, but needs to strive for wisdom and the ability to impart this wisdom.

Looking forward to the next stage, it is helpful to assist the Stage 2 believer explore options for service. The place for service is based on personal fit, not on organizational need, and this should be emphasized. Experimentation with finding that fit needs to be encouraged, and when adjustment is needed, it should never carry a tone of failure.

Chapter 5 Leadership Reflection:

God Is Good and the Original Creation Is Good!

> *And God said, "Let there be light," and there was light. And God saw that the light was good....*
>
> *God called the dry land Earth, and the waters that were gathered together he called Seas. And God saw that it was good. ...*

[27] Matthew 13:24–30

> *So God created man in his own image, in the image of God he created him; male and female he created them. ... And God saw everything that he had made, and behold, it was very good.* (Genesis 1:3, 10, 27–31 ESV)

Personal Reflection:

As we reflect on the wonder of the creation story and meditate on the goodness of God still visible throughout His creation, consider putting your thoughts on paper in answer to the following:

- Consider how the goodness of the Lord has manifested in your life. Write up a list of the times that God has been faithful to you over your lifetime.

- How has God's goodness manifested in the creation made a difference in your life?

- Write a prayer of praise and thanksgiving to God the Father as you review His history with you and the wonder of who He is.

Solomon's Praise!

God's Goodness, Love and Faithfulness!

> *O Lord, God of Israel, there is no God like you, in heaven or on earth, keeping covenant and showing steadfast love to your servants who walk before you with all their heart, who have kept with your servant David my father what you declared to him. You spoke with your mouth, and with your hand have fulfilled it this day.* (2 Chronicles 6:14–15 ESV)

Reflection of Praise and Thanksgiving:

- How has God's goodness influenced your direction in leadership?

- Can you receive encouragement in knowing that the goodness of God is manifested (albeit imperfectly) in your creativity and leadership endeavors? Consider jotting down some of these areas.

- Reflect on where God's goodness is manifesting in your work and personal life. Write a note of specific thanksgiving for the wonder of His presence in your life today.

Further Reflection:

Solomon's Prayer for Wisdom at the Start of His Ministry

> *Give your servant therefore an understanding mind to govern your people, that I may discern between good and evil, for who is able to govern this your great people?* (1 Kings 3:9 ESV)

Discerning Good and Evil: Our Good God Determines What is Good

> *And out of the ground the LORD God made to spring up every tree that is pleasant to the sight and good for food. The tree of life was in the midst of the garden, and the tree of the knowledge of good and evil.* (Genesis 2:9 ESV)

> *But the word is very near you. It is in your mouth and in your heart, so that you can do it. See, I have set before you today life and good, death and evil. ... Therefore choose life, that you and your offspring may live, loving the LORD your God, obeying his voice and holding fast to him, for he is your life.* (Deuteronomy 30:15–20 ESV)

In reading these passages, the fact is that God has full wisdom to determine good and evil, and it is His prerogative to make this determination. Usurping God's authority is something that is easily done. As a matter of fact, if we are honest with ourselves, we find it happens quite often.

- Make a note of the times when you have paused to discern God's wisdom and moved forward with a sense of peace and direction, and those times of an assumptive nature. The latter would be assuming one knows what is good and life giving because it seems right to us as we move in our self-motivated desires or through ungodly influence.

- How might slowing down for one-on-one time with God in priority setting or celebration impact "staying between the lanes" of one's walk being with God, rather than running ahead? Is there a difference to consider here? (Think about how it is if a journeyman apprentice moves out from under the guidance of a master.)

- Take a look at the times when you have sensed God closest. Is it while having a God talk when out in nature, or perhaps in the middle of a workout? Perhaps you have felt the closeness of His Presence while considering what it would have been like to be right there with the disciples when reading through the Gospels. Others find that getaways for quiet meditation open them up to God's direction, and lead to greater discernment.[28]

- Consider making greater margin and recreating environments that make more room for God time. What might this look like for you?

[28] Take a look at Adele Calhoun's (Calhoun, 2005) handbook for a variety of disciplines that can accomplish this.

Chapter 6:

The Sharing of Faith

This third stage of faith is one in which productivity is emphasized. Productivity in a personal relationship tends to be displayed as the active days of marriage, bringing children into the world and raising them up to be good people, and then releasing them into the world as independents. When we talk about productivity in a relationship with God and faith, we tend to talk about it in terms of active service in the church body. What this service looks like varies in function, depending on the focus a church may have, but all service should be clearly tied to doing or supporting the overall task of the Great Commission. Therefore, we are calling this stage the sharing of faith.

This line of sight to the Great Commission is quite important, as it keeps the service focused on working for God rather than on working for a person with charisma or a human vision with power. An individual's charisma will eventually be unmasked, the vision's power will fade, and the motive for service will be lost. God's task remains unchanged and focused.[29] The believer is encouraged to serve God, not to serve an organization or entity. This cannot be emphasized enough or repeated too many times; it needs to be deeply imbedded in the culture of the church.

This line of sight to the Great Commission is quite important, as it keeps the service focused on working for God rather than on working for a person with charisma or a human vision with power.

[29] Malachi 3:6

The overlap between Stage 2 (growth) and Stage 3 (sharing) is quite large. The early Stage 2 learner is also a novice Stage 3 producer. The nature of this stage is effective productivity based on knowing the right service fit and finding joy in the service activity or activities. At the beginning of this stage, a great deal of "service hopping" may be seen as the individual experiments with fit and personality. As we noted earlier, there should never be any sense of failure when a person finds that he or she is in a poor service fit, but a willing and smooth transition should be quickly encouraged. Jesus said, "My yoke is easy and my burden is light,"[30] and burdensome drudgery of service is a failure to understand and implement one of three things critical for effective and joyful service. Working through these three challenges is a major part of this stage of faith.

The first of these three challenges involves understanding and deepening the connection with God. Any relationship, including our relationship with God, is either growing or dying. Stasis is simply not an option, and any attempt to maintain a status quo will always result in decay and eventual relational death. As we apply this to our relationship with God, we see a strong and growing relationship in the first two stages of faith. As faith enters this productivity stage, however, we often see a tendency to replace the relationship with the work of productivity. In other words, productivity becomes an end unto itself, and the relational connection is no longer with the person of God, but with the work and byproducts of the work.

> A Scriptural principle we have found central to all of our lives as Christians is found in Ecclesiastes 7:18: "It is good to grasp the one and not let go of the other. The man who fears God will avoid all [extremes]" (NIV).

This, in and of itself, is not an apparent problem. The value of the work is not compromised by the motive behind the work. Often, in churches where labor for the work is in limited supply (we think that

30 Matthew 11:30

describes all of them!)[31] the temptation is to accept the volunteered efforts without asking too many questions. The issue lies in whether one is focused on the short-term organizational objectives of the church or the long-term spiritual health of the individual.

Without this balance, it is very hard for a human leader to avoid inflicting some level of spiritual abuse on members of the church.

Certainly, the short-term objectives of the church are not unimportant; a church cannot survive unless they are met. A leader of any organization must pay attention to these objectives and make sure they are either met or adjusted to ensure the viability of the organization. Yet, the fundamental purpose of the church is to disciple individuals, so the long-term spiritual health of an individual is also central to the organizational objective of the church. Keeping these two issues in balance is the key. A Scriptural principle we have found central to all of our lives as Christians is found in Ecclesiastes 7:18: "It is good to grasp the one and not let go of the other. The man who fears God will avoid all [extremes]" (NIV). Without this balance, it is very hard for a human leader to avoid inflicting some level of spiritual abuse on members of the church. A very good discussion of this issue and the need for balance is found in Ray Anderson's book on church leadership.[32] He explores the nature of authority and how it gets abused when a focus is singularly on the organizational or personal objectives of the leader.

When these goals are kept in balance, a leader will seek to explore and develop proper motives for ministry work. As we noted earlier in this chapter, it is critical that a focus is maintained that all ministry work is for God and not for the church or its leadership. The best way to develop this proper motivation is to keep the relationship with God growing. We have found that an introduction of the spiritual disciplines at this stage is most appropriate. While parts of these disciplines are involved in both of the earlier stages, it is not in a disciplined approach, but it is more of a function of passion. Introducing the concept of disciplines too early in the faith life can be detrimental and can risk making the disciplines a function of mere

[31] Matthew 9:37 (ESV): "Then he said to his disciples, 'The harvest is plentiful, but the laborers are few.'"

[32] Anderson, 1997

obedience instead of the function of growing a relationship with God.

It is not the scope of this book to discuss disciplines in detail; there are numerous books on the subject. There are three of note that we reference here for those who desire more information. The first is the classic work of Dallas Willard.[33] The second is the approach taken by Richard Foster.[34] The third is a comprehensive handbook written by Adele Ahlberg Calhoun.[35] Each of these appropriately places the role of disciplines in the arena of relationship, personal growth, and transformation.

It is important for the leader to assure that certain central purposes are being pursued as the individual exercises the disciplines. First, the purpose is to connect in a more powerful way with God. Second, it is imperative that the individual remains teachable before God, humble in one's humanity. Thirdly, the disciplines should be helping every person grow in understanding of God's identity and in one's identity as a child of God. A fourth purpose is to live out the Word, to put into practice what is being learned, and to walk the walk. Finally, the last focus is to begin to understand what is meant by praying continually, asking for guidance in everything, listening for God's promptings, and joining with God in His good pleasure and kingdom goals.

The second challenge to joyful service resides in failing to fully grasp and function in alignment with knowing one's self and how God has both gifted and designed an individual to work best. There are two things we look at here: personality styles and spiritual gifts. We delay assessment of these aspects until this stage, as both are primarily self-assessments that are based on previous attempts at service. There needs to be some history of service before any valid conclusions can be reached. There are a number of tools that can be used to aid in assessing these areas, most of them excellent. We believe one of the best is to be found at Uniquely You.[36]

[33] Willard, 1988

[34] Foster, 1988

[35] Calhoun, 2005

[36] www.uniquelyyou.org

> **The leader that values this aspect of the Body will seek to advocate for unity on a consistent basis. They will also keep "an ear to the ground" for any developing issues in this area. The leader will model and teach a style of assertive conflict resolution that avoids any sense of domination or inappropriate submissiveness.**

Aligning service to match one's personality and spiritual gifts, allows for service to be energizing and joy-filled. The opportunity to serve is positively anticipated, and the full person engages in it. Conversely, a mismatched opportunity leads to negative anticipation or dread, and limited energy is applied to the work itself. Note that the service is aligned to the individual, not the individual to the service. This is a critical difference to the leader. In the first case, the leader would set a direction for the church, and then would look for people to fill the roles necessary to that direction. In this second case, the leader looks at who the Lord has placed in his or her life and sets a direction based on who is available, ready, and willing to serve. This approach helps us to discern how God wants us to lead far more effectively than the first approach.

The third challenge to joyful service lies in our relationships to each other. Specifically, we are looking at how well the community of the church is implementing Jesus' command to love one another.[37] When a community loves well, there is active and healthy forgiveness displayed within the Body, an intentional focus on releasing hurts and finding peace. When the community is struggling in this area, service is not a good experience, as those we serve with are not those we love and for whom we desire good things. Instead, we get more focused on how to avoid being hurt, or in more extreme cases, how to inflict hurt on those we should be in unity with.

The leader that values this aspect of the Body will seek to advocate for unity on a consistent basis. This person will also keep "an ear to the ground" for any developing issues in this area. The leader will model and teach a style of assertive conflict resolution that avoids any sense of domination or inappropriate submissiveness. Jesus taught this model, and we find it in Matthew 18:15–20. When a church can

[37] John 13:34–35

effectively and appropriately implement this into the culture of the church, great movement toward unity and service is gained.

This stage of productivity is the most recognizable stage to our American churches. It is the stage upon which many churches are built. And, when it is functioning with the motives in the proper place (or moving toward the proper place), it is a place of excitement and great joy. It is the church of Acts!

Chapter 6 Leadership Reflection:

Paul's Productivity: The Preparation of Paul and His Call to the Gentiles

As we consider the productive stage of faith, one of the most productive leaders recorded in the Bible is Paul. Prior to Paul beginning his Christ-centered ministry, he spent up to three years in personally receiving Christ's revelations. Though he was a highly educated Jew in his own right, he counted it all as rubbish compared to the glory of these revelations (Philippians 3:8).

> *Am I now trying to win the approval of human beings, or of God? Or am I trying to please people? If I were still trying to please people, I would not be a servant of Christ. I want you to know, brothers and sisters, that the gospel I preached is not of human origin. I did not receive it from any man, nor was I taught it; rather, I received it by revelation from Jesus Christ. ... But when God, who set me apart from my mother's womb and called me by his grace, was pleased to reveal his Son in me so that I might preach him among the Gentiles, my immediate response was not to consult any human being. I did not go up to Jerusalem to see those who were apostles before I was, but I went into Arabia. Later I returned to Damascus. Then after three years, I went up to Jerusalem.* (Galatians 1:11–18 NIV)

Personal Reflection:

- How did God prepare you for the leadership of the people you have been given?

- Is there a specific call on your life? What might that call be?

Paul's Productivity Enhanced: Imprisoned for the Gospel

> *For two whole years Paul stayed there in his own rented house and welcomed all who came to see him. Boldly and without hindrance he preached the kingdom of God and taught about the LORD Jesus Christ.* (Acts 28:30–31 NIV)

- Have there been confining circumstances in your life that in retrospect, resulted in a furtherance of God's kingdom purposes? Perhaps, you are in that confinement now. Describe what that has been or is like for you.

- How might understanding the stages of faith assist you at these times?

The Active Life of Christ

Now, let us consider Christ Himself. In the Gospel testimonies, Christ began His ministry with 40 days in seclusion in the wilderness (Matthew 4:1–11). He frequented desolate places to spend time with His father (Luke 5:16). These times of solitude and prayer were particularly noted before times of direction setting (Matthew 4:1–11, Matthew 17:1–9, and Luke 6:12); following energy-intensive gatherings (Matthew 14:23, Mark 1:35, Mark 6:31, and Luke 5:16); and during personal times of grief and angst (Matthew 14:13 and Matthew 2:36–46).

- What teachings does Jesus exemplify in maintaining an active ministry life?

- How might your leadership and leadership team benefit from building similar patterns into ministry routine in order to encourage discernment and continued productivity for the kingdom?

Further Reflection:

Come Get Some Rest

Read this passage three times slowly, and allow it to speak into your life:

> *Then, because so many people were coming and going that they did not even have a chance to eat, he said to them, "Come with me by yourselves to a quiet place and get some rest."* (Mark 6:31 NIV)

- After the repetitive meditation, consider this question: "What invitation does Jesus have for me personally with these words of life?"

- Do you have space and times set in place to assure that you can get away and rest with Jesus? What are your thoughts here?

Chapter 7:

The Blessing of Disillusionment

We live in a broken world, and we are subject to the imbalance that was wrought upon all creation in the Fall. The imperfections are pervasive, impacting all interactions, including how we think and feel. We were created with purpose, and all that we were created for still resides in us as desires and longings. Intuitively we know that the world that we experience is not right, and we chafe against our inability to achieve those desires that are so deeply imbedded within us. Yet even the desires seem to be imperfectly understood in our broken states, and we end up both interpreting and pursuing them in ways that are contrary to God's original design.

There is much to be explored on this topic, and much of it is beyond the scope of this book. Bruce Demarest refers to this stage as times of painful disorientation. He identifies three parts to this time: seasons of distress, seasons of understanding why we suffer, and seasons of the dark night of the soul.[38] Benedict Groeschel identifies it as a time of purgation.[39] Os Guiness writes about it as a time of doubting.[40] Gary Thomas writes about it as a time of sin and temptation.[41] It could also be called a time of disillusionment when God does not live up to who we thought Him to be, nor does He do what we thought

[38] Demarest, 2009

[39] Groeschel, 1999

[40] Guiness, 1996

[41] Thomas, 2001

He would do. This might include us having to take up our cross in such life events as disturbing changes or loss of the status quo; disastrous events in our community, work, or family; disease striking ourselves or our loved ones; depression as things don't turn out the way we had hoped; the death of those we care about or the possibility of our own death; and finally, an accumulation of challenges that become despair.

> Intuitively we know that the world that we experience is not right, and we chafe against our inability to achieve those desires that are so deeply imbedded within us.

For the purposes of understanding leadership in this place of brokenness and Godly desires, it is enough to understand that a life that is growing closer in relationship to God, that is beginning to join with Him in His kingdom goals and His purposes, will inevitably experience deep disillusionment. This disillusionment will get focused on others, self, and even on God. It often manifests as anger and frustration. It questions the value of service toward a seemingly unattainable goal, and those in this stage of faith are keenly aware of how truly far from God's purposes they are.

We have seen so many times in our experience as counselors and church leaders that the interpretation of this stage by both the individuals and those surrounding them is that it is a loss of faith. Then all focus is to lead them back to Stage 2 or Stage 3 activities in the hope of reigniting the passions that had been experienced there. This invariably is simply unsuccessful, and in some cases, results in the actual loss of faith. More often, it leads the individual to withdraw from service, to hesitate to engage in the spiritual disciplines, and to question whether such activities are even appropriate.

The damage we have seen inflicted on those in this stage has led us to call this stage "the blessing of disillusionment." It is a blessing, though it is a very difficult time to experience. It is critical that the leader both expect this stage and embrace it as a normal and valuable stage of growth. Properly handled, this stage moves the individual to a deeper level of surrender to God and a deeper and more abiding peace based on His goodness. Improperly handled, it labels the individual as flawed in faith and creates a long-lasting angst of identity.

> We call this stage "the blessing of disillusionment." It is a blessing, though it is a very difficult time to experience. It is critical that the leader both expect this stage and embrace it as a normal and valuable stage of growth.

We conflate two of the stages used by Hagberg and Guelich[42] into one here. We find that the stage of disillusionment and the stage of resolution are essentially parts of the same stage. Asking and resolving deep questions of faith are what constitutes it. The leader can help this stage by clarifying the underlying questions and by pointing the way toward a resolution. Again, embracing this stage as an important part of growth cannot be overemphasized.

In order to bring these questions to light, a leader needs to have some insight into what the central questions of this stage might be. We have found that there are four questions that repeatedly emerge with individuals experiencing disillusionment. These four questions are related to one another, and they center on the basic character of God.

The first of these questions is the least directly related to God. The question can be stated as, "How can I be calm in the face of so much unknown?" This question is all about fear of the unknown, and it becomes debilitating to some. Foundationally, fear is controlled when we believe we have some level of control or some sense of safety and security in life. Fear grows out of proportion to the actual danger when that sense is lost. Sometimes, the best starting place is to label fear for what it is: simply fear. Then the individual can start to assess the reality of the fear and what the alternatives are.

> Central questions that must be resolved in this stage are:
> - How can I be calm in the face of so much unknown?
> - Can I really trust God with my life?
> - Is God really good?

[42] Hagberg and Guelich, 2005

- If He is good, then can He be sovereign, when my life is going in the direction it is?

When we talk about fear and the sense of safety and security, we next progress to the questions more directly related to God. "Can I really trust God with my life?" is a significant question at this point. Some level of experience is telling them that God is not necessarily trustworthy, at least not to provide what they feel is necessary to safety and security. This experience is concretely real and should not be dismissed as a lack of faith. Instead, the experience should be validated and explored. Often, lying underneath the question of trust is this question: "Is God really good?" A fourth question that relates to this also shows up. This question revolves around God's sovereignty: "If He is good, then can He be sovereign, when my life is going in the direction it is?"

Many times we have found that these questions are hidden beneath others that seem more acceptable. It seems that we (the Christian community) can teach that the questions we are talking about are sacrilegious to ask, or even think. When this pressure is in place, the questions are avoided directly, but the issues remain unresolved. In the attempt to resolve the issues, many false trails are followed. Revealing these trails as false leads and giving permission to ask these central questions are the roles of the leader, at this point.

When the central questions are out in the open and accepted as central by the individual, the leader may start to point toward the path to resolution. It is so important that the leader does not simply give what he or she perceives to be the answer but only points out the path. One of the best ways to do this is by asking more questions. If God is sovereign, is He allowing this time of struggle for a purpose? Can we know that purpose? Might He choose to hide that purpose from us for a time? How is God's goodness made manifest in His Son? Can that goodness override these worldly concerns? What does loving God and others look like in this current situation? How might the goodness and glory of God be revealed in that expression of love?

It needs to be kept in mind that the surrender God seeks is not a surrender in the sense of a war. It is, instead, a willing surrender of self to the recognized greater good of God and His purposes.

All individuals must work out their specific answers to these questions for themselves. If the foundations of the earlier stages of faith have been well set, this process will work out with a movement toward a surrender of self. It needs to be kept in mind that the surrender God seeks is not a surrender in the sense of a war. It is, instead, a willing surrender of self to the recognized greater good of God and His purposes. This surrender cannot fully take place if the questions of disillusionment are current without resolution.

We are offering a way to walk through this surrender process in Appendix C of this book. It is certainly not the only way this can be done, but it is one way that has been very helpful for some. A key component of this process is confession and forgiveness.

A final thought on this stage addresses the need to allow for mystery. God ways are not our ways, and His thoughts are not our thoughts.[43] Accepting that God is bigger than our minds can grasp and that His plans are from a perspective we cannot see helps us to surrender to His ways. Not all questions can be answered, but that does not mean they cannot be resolved. Learning to hold those questions in the tension between answers and the goodness of God is a gift of the journey through this stage.

Chapter 7 Leadership Reflection:

[44]Who Is Your Hero?

The Bible is full of heroic leaders who came face to face with the depth of earthly challenge, brokenness, and disillusionment. These challenges are often called the "desert experiences" of this life. Following is a review of a few of them.

---

43 Isaiah 55:8

44 We expanded the "reflection" section of this stage and included some resources for guidance in appendices, as this one seems the most difficult for leaders to work with. We pray that these reflections/meditations will provide some tools and experience to help others navigate these troubled but blessed waters.

In the Old Testament, Abraham awaited the birth of his son of promise, Isaac, for 25 years and then was asked to sacrifice him. David was pursued by Saul for at least seven years, knowing that he would become king upon Saul's death. Elijah, having stood in faith with great strength, faced his wall when he was chased by the army of Jezebel. Moses, Joshua, and Caleb had their 40 years in the desert before reaching the Promised Land. Joseph was in prison for 10 years before beginning service to the Pharaoh of Egypt. (For further examples, see **Appendix A** for an indepth look at the sanctifying journeys of three of the early kings.)

Moving on to the New Testament, James and John insisted that they were to be at the right and left hands of Jesus as he came into His kingdom, even though God already had plans for who would be seated there. As we know, these disciples faced trial upon trial in choosing to be baptized with Jesus' baptism and to drink from the depth of Jesus' cup. Finally, we focus on Paul who persecuted Christians, even to their death. Following his conversion, he spent three years under the tutelage of Christ, most likely in desert places.

- What call of heroism or sacrifice has God placed upon your life? Have you found that these times of challenge deepen your relationship with Him or create more of a dividing wall?

- What kinds of thoughts do you have at times of deep challenge? Do these thoughts contain truth or lies? The thoughts will come either from yourself and your history, from God, or from the enemy. Which of these do your thoughts come from? (Consider setting aside time in discerning what your battle at the wall is. **See Appendix B** for an approach to develop this.)

- How might your leadership and leadership team benefit from understanding the blessing of disillusionment to encourage them in what one might call "walking through the darkness to see His light"? How might this understanding empower those you serve in walking their journey of faith as they come up against the "walls" in their lives?

Leadership Reflection Two:

Job and the Elusive Blessing of Disillusionment

As we consider the depth of difficulty faced at this stage of faith, we look at the story of Job. Job faced intense disillusionment with a series of calamities that led to the loss of all that was important and meaningful in his life. This included disastrous losses of his livestock, his property, and the death and thus loss of relationship with all his children. He was also overcome with disease. These circumstances led to eventual rejection by his wife, loss of his standing in his community, and finally deep disrespect from his friends. Job grieved and cried out to God in frustration, even despairing of life.

The one thing Job hung onto was his relationship with God. Only a close connection with our Creator/Father could keep one going during those kinds of hard times. Job had to truly know the goodness, worthiness, and faithfulness of God. His perspective became even more clear as he experienced the depth of his own fallibility in contrast to our Great God.

Consider the following scriptures as they elaborate upon the relationship between God and Job:

> *In the land of Uz there lived a man whose name was Job. This man was blameless and upright; he feared God and shunned evil. ... When a period of feasting had run its course, Job would send and have them [his children] purified. Early in the morning he would*

sacrifice a burnt offering for each of them, thinking, "Perhaps my children have sinned and cursed God in their hearts." This was Job's regular custom. ...

Then the LORD said to Satan, "Have you considered my servant Job? There is no one on earth like him; he is blameless and upright, a man who fears God and shuns evil." ...

And [Job] said: "Naked I came from my mother's womb, and naked I will depart. The LORD gave and the LORD has taken away; may the name of the LORD be praised. ... Shall we accept good from God, and not trouble?" In all this, Job did not sin in what he said. ... "I loathe my very life; therefore I will give free rein to my complaint and speak out in the bitterness of my soul. ... Though he slay me, yet will I hope in him; I will surely defend my ways to his face. ... I know that my Redeemer lives, and that in the end he will stand upon the earth."

... The LORD said to Job: "Will the one who contends with the Almighty correct him? Let him who accuses God answer him!" ...

Then Job answered the LORD: "I am unworthy—how can I reply to you? I put my hand over my mouth." (Job 1:1, 5, 8, 21; 2:10; 10:1; 13:15; 19:25; 40:1–4 NIV).

Personal Reflection:

- How is your relationship going with God right now? Has Christ become the friend you can lean on and our Father the strong tower to run to? Has the presence of the Spirit prompted and given you direction?

- What would happen if you faced even two or three of Job's losses (perhaps you have)? Would it be difficult to believe that the Godhead is good or that He personally has your back?

- Further, what would it be like to lose everything, including your own wellbeing? Would God be enough? Would you be or are you willing to lay your complaints before God as Job did?

- How does the knowledge of God's goodness, worthiness, and faithfulness speak into these challenges? How does the depth of God's sacrifice and the wonderment of him laying out his own Son on that cross impact our willingness to draw close to God in all circumstances?

Further Reflection:

Biblical Invitation to Lay Our Complaints before the Lord

As we follow in the example of the complaints of Job, the journals of David (particularly the Imprecatory Psalms), the Lamentations of Jeremiah, and the cries of Asaph in Psalm 73 (see Appendix B), we are directed to lay out our frustrations and heartaches as well as our joys and thanksgiving before the Lord. As we cry out to the Lord, we give sacrifice and thanksgiving for all that our Godhead has done for us with authenticity and integrity.

We find that as we "contend" with God, we gain momentum in understanding and trust in the depth of who our Godhead truly is. We find answers or have peace about the questions we do not know what to do with. We find that our faith grows and that His faithfulness is magnified.

Job and the Blessing of Disillusionment

> *In all this, Job did not sin by charging God with wrongdoing. ... "Shall we receive good from God, and shall we not receive evil?" ... In all of this Job did not sin with his lips. ... "I loathe my very life; therefore I will give free rein to my complaint and speak out in the bitterness of my soul."*

(Review the long discourse of Job's complaints and his claim of faithfulness to God intermixed with the commentaries of those he called friends.)

> *The LORD said to Job: "Will the one who contends with the Almighty correct him? Let him who accuses God answer him!" ...*
>
> *Then Job answered the LORD: "I am unworthy—how can I reply to you? I put my hand over my mouth. ... I know that you can do all things, and that no purpose of yours can be thwarted. I had heard of you by the hearing of the ear, but now my eye sees you, therefore I despise myself, and repent in dust and ashes." ...*
>
> *After the LORD had said these things to Job, he said to [his friends] ... "I am angry with you and your two friends, because you have not spoken of me what is right, as my servant Job has. ... My servant Job will pray for you, and I will accept his prayer and not deal with you according to your folly. You have not spoken of me what is right, as my servant Job has." ... and the LORD accepted Job's prayer. ... After Job had prayed for his friends, the LORD made him prosperous again and gave him twice as much as he had before. ...*
>
> *The LORD blessed the latter part of Job's life more than the first. ... And so he died, old and full of years.* (Job 1:22; 2:9–10; 10:1; 40:1–4; 42:2, 5–6; 42:12, 17 NIV)

- What are the complaints that are hiding in your heart these days? How does this impact yourself, your family, your ministry, and your community?

- Would you be willing to live with the decision to write out the challenges (and victories) to the Lord, knowing that you are following in the footsteps of the "man after God's own heart"?

- Is there a mentor, mentor group, spiritual director, or Christian counselor who could encourage you on this journey?

See **Appendix B** to go deeper into Asaph's journey through oppression.

Chapter 8:

Living the Call

This last stage of faith is greater peace.[45] In this stage, we live out the call of God in our lives without insisting on our own agendas. We cannot say "maturity," because full maturity this side of heaven is impossible. It is also inaccurate to call the earlier stages immature. Instead, it is better to see this stage as a key milestone in the journey. It is a place to stop, enjoy, and rest as we get prepared to begin the next part of the journey.

In at least one way, this can look like the first stage of faith. The enthusiasm of that stage is recaptured as many of the questions that challenge our faith are resolved (not necessarily answered, but resolved). One can now look at a relationship with God and service to the kingdom with a great deal of joy and understanding. This enthusiasm is often seen as passion for the character of God and the purpose of His work.

Resolving the tough faith questions of the stage of disillusionment gives one a much greater sense of the depth of who God is—and who He is not. In this place, God does not appear capricious or vengeful, but loving and purposeful. It is no longer troubling that God does not act in an apparent consistent manner, predictable to the analysis of humanity. There is peace in allowing God to be God and us to be His creation.

A relationship with God is seen as a treasure to be nourished and deepened without placing demands or expectations on Him to be

[45] Hagberg and Guelich, 2005

someone we can fully understand. This work of relationship may look similar in some ways to earlier stages, but it now lacks the drive of individual need and allows God to set the direction and timing of growth.

> A relationship with God is seen as a treasure to be nourished and deepened without placing demands or expectations on Him to be someone we can fully understand.

Individuals who have worked through the earlier stages and are now here, also possess a much greater sense of their own identity. While still not complete, they have a strong sense of their own giftings, their own strengths, and both an understanding and acceptance of their own failings. This balance of understanding reveals itself in a gentle humility. True humility does not deny their giftings and strengths; it simply understands these to be gifts from God that should be used for His glory. Any good that results from using these gifts and strengths is a direct consequence of God's goodness and is attributed to Him accordingly. The understanding of their own failings acts as a check on the pride that tempts them when they are used by God. They become aware that, left alone, they are most likely to mess things up and will need rescuing. Therefore, reliance on God in all areas of life is seen as critical.

In this stage, these believers also have a keen sense of how God desires to use them individually in His kingdom. They come to see their unique role in the kingdom as a part of a whole, a truer understanding of the Body of Christ. For some, it can now be acceptable to simply shape a few people for God. Or, for others, it may be clear that crowds are the work God has for them. The venue for God to be revealed through His work in each individual is both understood and accepted.

One result is that individuals in this stage are quite self-directed (or God-directed is better). They do not simply fall into programmatic visions of a church and find a place to fit. Instead, they tend to look for the place that best matches how they understand God is leading them. From the outside, this can look unfocused and even confused. We have seen that God has a tendency to lead in a circuitous path, with many ups and downs, twists and turns, and even the occasional sudden 90-degree turn. Those who have reached this stage move in concert with God on this journey and allow Him to lead.

Leaders who understand this stage will seek to recognize those individuals that God has brought into their midst and will look to adjust their vision to fit the call on their lives. When that adjustment would violate the clear calling of the leader, a loving and empowering release to another part of the Body is made. Both elements are key here; the release must be both loving and empowering. Loving will acknowledge the value of God's call on the individual and the value God has placed on each one. Love will affirm what God is doing and will pass no judgment. Empowering will look to assist the individual to find the right place in the greater Body. It will not be a simple dismissal and goodbye.

It is so important to remember that this stage is not an endpoint, but really just another beginning point. God is limitless, and in our relationship with Him, we are called to new levels of growth, education, and production. Invariably, these new levels will lead to new disillusionments and new resolutions. As we noted earlier in the book, we see the stages of faith as a spiral, a view shared by quite a few others.[46] We need to always keep in mind that we are neither in front of nor behind anyone in these stages. We are where we are, and we will be where others are at some point in the future.

From the outside, this stage can look unfocused and even confused. We have seen God has a tendency to lead in a circuitous path, with many ups and downs, twists and turns, and even the occasional sudden 90-degree turn.

Chapter 8 Leadership Reflection:

On the Transforming Path with Abraham

As we follow hard after God, our confidence grows in our relationship with him through Christ. We see this in the journeys of the saints that have gone before us.

[46] Demarest, 2009; Fowler, 1981; Groeschel, 1999

Consider Abraham and his initial fear and lack of trust in God. In his early travels, Abraham took things into his own hands and stated that his wife was his sister (she was his half-sister) rather than claiming her as his wife. Though Abraham was following God's direction to his promised land, he didn't have the confidence in God and chose to protect his own person rather than rely on God.

> *Now Abraham moved on from there into the region of the Negev and lived between Kadesh and Shur. For a while he stayed in Gerar, and there Abraham said of his wife Sarah, "She is my sister." Then Abimelech king of Gerar sent for Sarah and took her.*
>
> *But God came to Abimelech in a dream one night and said to him, "You are as good as dead because of the woman you have taken; she is a married woman."...*
>
> *Abraham replied, "I said to myself, 'There is surely no fear of God in this place, and they will kill me because of my wife.'"* (Genesis 20:1–3, 11, NIV)

In following his story, we see the progression. After years of being conformed, being transformed, and of gaining greater experience and understanding of unseen reality through his relationship with God, Abraham was so confident in Him that he was willing to sacrifice his promised son, Isaac, on an altar to God.

Note Abraham's transformation of faith:

> *Some time later God tested Abraham. He said to him, "Abraham!"*
>
> *"Here I am," he replied.*
>
> *Then God said, "Take your son, your only son, whom you love—Isaac—and go to the region of Moriah. Sacrifice him there as a burnt offering on a mountain I will show you." ...*
>
> *He said to his servants, "Stay here with the donkey while I and the boy go over there. We will worship and then we will come back to you."*
>
> *Abraham took the wood for the burnt offering and placed it on his son Isaac, and he himself carried the fire and the knife. As the two*

of them went on together, Isaac spoke up and said to his father Abraham, "Father?"

"Yes, my son?" Abraham replied.

"The fire and wood are here," Isaac said, "but where is the lamb for the burnt offering?" ...

Then he reached out his hand and took the knife to slay his son. But the angel of the LORD called out to him from heaven, "Abraham! Abraham!"

"Here I am," he replied.

"Do not lay a hand on the boy," he said. "Do not do anything to him. Now I know that you fear God, because you have not withheld from me your son, your only son." (Genesis 22:1–2, 5–7, 10–12, NIV)

Personal Reflection:

- What are the times when God has tested you in your leadership walk or, perhaps, one might call it a marathon? During what aspects of the sojourn has it been easy to trust God? When has it been difficult?

- Consider writing down a timeline of the testing of your faith. Note the challenges, the areas of strength, and the areas of perceived weakness, and then note the strength gained over time in your relationship with God.

- Take a look at the difference between where your faith was at in five- to ten-year segments. What is the difference between where you were as you began your relationship with the Godhead and where you are at in your faith today?

- How does understanding the stages of faith add to the understanding of your faith history? Might this exercise be helpful for your leadership team or others you serve?

Paul on Discernment and the Furthering of the Faith

Paul went through repeated ups and downs on his journey of faith, as a persecutor of Christians, during his conversion experience, and throughout his ministry of proclaiming the Gospel. He acknowledged the depth of his passion in seeking after God, his deeply imbedded connection to Christ, and his heart to reveal God's glory through the Holy Spirit.

Paul's intimacy with God and His Word is unquestionable. He exemplified a life filled with consistent discernment through prayer rooted in praise for God and grounded in thanksgiving and concern for believers. He encouraged gathering in community for himself and for the building up of the Body. His writings are an inspired expression of God's love and caring for the world through the closeness of Paul's relationship with God.

Reflect on these passages and note what stands out to you:

> *Grace to you and peace from God our Father and the LORD Jesus Christ, who gave himself for our sins to deliver us from the present evil age, according to the will of our God and Father, to whom be the glory forever and ever. Amen. ...*

For am I now seeking the approval of man, or of God? Or am I trying to please man? If I were still trying to please man, I would not be a servant of Christ.

For I would have you know, brothers, that the gospel that was preached by me is not man's gospel. For I did not receive it from any man, nor was I taught it, but I received it through a revelation of Jesus Christ. ...

But when he who had set me apart before I was born, and who called me by his grace, was pleased to reveal his Son to me, in order that I might preach him among the Gentiles, I did not immediately consult with anyone; nor did I go up to Jerusalem to those who were apostles before me, but I went away into Arabia, and returned again to Damascus.

Then after three years I went up to Jerusalem. ... And they glorified God because of me. (Galatians 1:3–5, 10–12, 15–18, 24, ESV)

Further Reflection:

Whatever Situation and In All Things

Paul made it clear that his confidence had grown strong in the faith through his attunement to Christ and in dedication to discernment with the Lord.

Meditate upon the following passages slowly repeating the reading three times as follows:

- 1st READING: Focus on the content.
- 2nd READING: Note the verses that stand out to you during this reading.
- 3rd READING: Consider what deepened understanding, invitation to further discernment, or call to action is inspired in you through the reading of these passages.

Do not be conformed to this world, but be transformed by the renewal of your mind, that by testing you may discern what is the will of God, what is good and acceptable and perfect. (Romans 12:2 ESV)

> *Not that I am speaking of being in need, for I have learned in whatever situation I am to be content. I know how to be brought low, and I know how to abound. In any and every circumstance, I have learned the secret of facing plenty and hunger, abundance and need. I can do all things through him who strengthens me.* (Philippians 4:11–13 ESV)

- Consider journaling in answer to this question: "How do conformation, transformation, and the renewal of the mind connect with the discernment of God's will?"

- What are those "things" that God has called you to or might be preparing you to do in which spending time in discernment could strengthen your leadership?

- In view of understanding the stages of faith, how can you encourage those you serve in the areas of their calling?

Chapter 9:

Leading Beyond Limits

Summary of Stages

Stage	Our Label	Primary Characteristic	Movement to Next Stage
Stage 1	Beginning of Faith	Enthusiasm	Healing of hurts
Stage 2	Growth of Faith	Hunger for knowledge	Apprenticing
Stage 3	Sharing of Faith	Productivity	Unmet expectations and desires
Stage 4	Blessing of disillusionment	Disillusionment and working out resolution	Willingness to accept that some questions are unanswerable
Stage 5	Living the Call	Peace	New insight
Return to Stage 1: Fresh perspectives leading to new levels of enthusiasm and a reengagement of the spiral of the stages			

Larry Crabb wrote a book in 1999 in which he painted a vision of what the church could be. In an opening statement, he says this: "As we debate the differences between therapy, spiritual direction, lay counseling, and discipleship, we really should admit that we don't quite know what we're talking about. Neither the goal toward which we are aiming (exactly what does it mean to be whole, to be mature) nor the process of getting there is clearly understood by anyone."[47]

[47] Crabb, 1999

This statement is still true today, and it certainly it applies to this book. We have ideas, and those ideas are based on research and experience, but they are not fully developed answers.

What leadership looks like when we grasp the whole concept of how we grow and develop in our faith and how that process is a never-ending cycle is not completely clear. Like Larry Crabb, we have a vision of what a true spiritual community can look like based on this. And as he states in his book, we should not expect it to be easy. However, there are certain principles and key approaches that we can suggest. Some are new and some are not. Some are obscure and some are blazingly obvious. We believe that compiling these here can benefit leaders and help start a conversation on how we do that which Christ called upon his disciples to do—love one another.[48]

The first and most important principle the leader needs to embrace is fairly obvious, but it is not often practiced. This principle is that each stage has something to offer the Body, and the Body is incomplete without each stage's contributions. The Apostle Paul's teachings on the body of many parts are applicable here as well as toward spiritual giftings.[49] Insightful leaders will honor and celebrate each stage. They will work to establish a place for each stage in the church life. They will engage others for the purpose of building up the Body. And very critically, they need to be watchful for the arrival of judgmentalism and pride, and be quick to address it.

We are quick to say here that this does not mean every church must be everything to everyone. If that were the case, we would be doomed to failure, since that is both intuitively and practically impossible. When we say that every church needs to find a place for members in each stage, we are saying that each church's vision needs to be broad enough to encompass the benefits that each stage and each individual bring to each particular church. With this in mind, we will look at how a leader might both use and empower those in each stage for the furtherance of the kingdom and building up of the Body.

---

[48] John 13:35

[49] 1 Corinthians 12:12–20

> **The first and most important principle the leader needs to embrace is fairly obvious, but it is not often practiced. This principle is that each stage has something to offer the Body and the Body is incomplete without each stage's contributions.**

As we discussed in Chapter 4, the first stage is best characterized by enthusiasm. This authentic enthusiasm needs to be captured and made a part of the church culture. There are many ways this can be done. Encouraging testimonials from these Stage 1 individuals is a great way to do this, but it often risks an unfocused message. In this day and age of easy video and editing, this risk can be managed without too much effort. Engage a volunteer to develop these videos and help them focus them on the central message of joy. Another way to imbed the church with a culture of authentic enthusiasm is to allow guests to come speak at various settings of the church including Bible studies, small groups, and leadership meetings. Leadership encouragement of the expression of how the members see God at work and the joy of Him in life will see this type of expression grow and flourish.

Since this first stage of faith is often in need of some level of emotional, spiritual, or psychological healing (lines get blurred here), it is good to make sure the church either sets up the healing venues we discussed in Chapter 4 or has a solid referral to Christian sources for this healing to occur. Here it is crucial that leadership is communicating the need and value for such healing and the venues being offered. If attendance at such venues is perceived as outside of the church function and purpose in any way, the individuals attending will end up feeling marginalized and less than valuable members of the Body. We have seen leaders who proclaim their own need of this healing and its value, instilling this culture in the church.

Helpers and mentors for these venues of healing can be drawn from members in Stages 2, 3, and 5. Stages 3 and 5 members can be especially helpful, as they are more fully equipped and most likely understand their unique giftedness to serve in these areas. Stage 5 members are especially good at inciting a catalytic growth of the expression of joy in the relationship with God.

Finally, it is good to encourage these first stage members to begin to engage in service opportunities as assistants and helpers. They are usually not ready to take on full leadership responsibilities, but engagement in various ministry functions allows them to taste and test how God is gifting and calling them to serve. It also allows them another venue to impart the enthusiasm that is so valuable.

The second stage member is best characterized by a desire to learn. The leader will want to ensure that appropriate learning environments are encouraged. All of these do not need to be formal classes, though they can certainly be a part of embracing this stage. Some leaders can be mentors to individuals or groups of up to three. Teachers and mentors can be drawn from members in Stages 3 and 5 and targeted to very specific interest areas. Deemphasizing class size can help make sure the needs of all the Stage 2 learners are being met. We have taught a year-long through the Bible class to as few as six attendees, yet have seen big changes in the culture of the church as a result. If the church is very small, it is important to encourage attendance at studies of other churches that can offer these educational opportunities. Having a mindset of noncompetition with other churches can aid the proper understanding of the whole church as the Body of Christ.

Our current church models are actually very good at empowering the production stage of faith. What is sometimes lacking is the assurance that the motive for this production is focused on the kingdom and God's glory. The centrality of evangelism needs to be emphasized, along with discipleship for the purpose of building up the Body of Christ. These Stage 3 members are the productive life of the church and are usually most visible. The celebration of service should not be lessened but broadened to include areas of service that are sometimes not as visible. Finding and celebrating the behind-the-scenes service goes a long way toward helping to assure proper motivations. The leader cannot be afraid to impact service by asking wrongly motivated individuals to stand back and reevaluate why they serve. Another option is to partner a Stage 3 member with a Stage 5 member in service. The Stage 5 member's understanding of the function and true source of joy in service will tend to rub off on the Stage 3 producer.

A final thought for this stage of sharing, is to make sure the members are introduced to the ideas of spiritual gifting and personality traits that they might possess. Find an inventory that is easy to administer and target its completion to those in this stage. Our experience is that it will need to be redone in this stage if it was completed earlier. The answers received will change with greater involvement in the work of the church.

Our hearts are soft toward the disillusioned Stage 4 members. We feel this stage is essential to the full maturity of the Body of Christ, and we have seen it condemned so many times. Yet, it is the nature of any relationship to experience disillusionment, and our relationship with God is no different. When one perseveres through disillusionment and fights for resolution of these faith challenging questions, the joy of service and depth of relationship is unparalleled by anything else in this world.

Stage 4 members should not be used in service roles without Stage 5 partners. If paired with a Stage 3 member, the tendency is toward the sharing of the disillusionment instead of vice versa. When partnered with a Stage 5 member, guidance can be given from experience on how to fight for resolution. We recommend one-on-one mentoring at this stage with someone who can hear the faith challenge, can accept it as normal and growth oriented, and can point the direction of resolution. This is a time of reflection and soul searching, and the leader can help by advising and assisting the individual to make time for it and not allow busyness to distract from it.

The leader would do well to identify and hold up the Stage 5 members in their midst as the holders of wisdom. Wisdom is not greater knowledge, but greater insight. Individuals who have journeyed through disillusionment and found resolution do not have all the answers, but they do have a great deal of insight. Because humility is a feature of this stage, a comfort level with being held up in this manner is not to be expected. However, the leader needs to insist that wisdom has been obtained and there is valuable information to share. Recruiting mentors from this population should be a high priority of any leader.

A couple of final thoughts on leading beyond limits are in order. It seems to us there is a choice in leadership direction here. One can choose to cast a vision and then seek to find those who can assist in achieving that vision. This choice is a decision to engage in a worldly perspective of limited resources, limited manpower, limited finances, and limited engagement. Such a plan will ultimately lead to competitiveness within the Body of Christ as the leader seeks a share of these limited resources. Any attempt by the leader to be everything to everyone will eventually result in overwhelm and burnout.

> The leader must choose between a kingdom of limited resources and competition or God's kingdom of unlimited resources and cooperation.

The other choice, the one we feel can be found by following the principles we have laid out here, leads to the engagement of the unlimited resources of God's kingdom. The leader needs to have a keen sense of one's own stage of faith and a mentor who is helping him or her move along the journey. That mentor must be chosen carefully based on a history of successful mentoring of other leaders through the stages of faith.

Leaders who are implementing and empowering each stage will adjust the focus of the church to match the people God has drawn to it. Leaders beyond limits empower others in each and every stage. Manpower is increased, and the church atmosphere is one of excited service. Leaders at this point are really followers of what God is placing in their paths. This engagement will, in turn, empower leaders to lead beyond their own limits, finding and using the unlimited resources of God's kingdom.

So, what are the next steps? We have included a possible format (Appendix D) for walking through this book with a leadership team and applying it to your specific ministry setting. If you choose this option, it is important to allow the material time to settle in and soak. Be sure you allow this time and do not rush the process of the Spirit working in you as individuals and as a group.

It is our prayer that this book has provided some meat to chew on for leaders of churches. It is also recognized that these principles can be applied in any discipleship setting, and we hope that it ignites some discussion and movement within the greater Body of Christ. We do not have the final answers, but we see this as a place to begin some new or to renew some old conversations. To God alone be all glory.

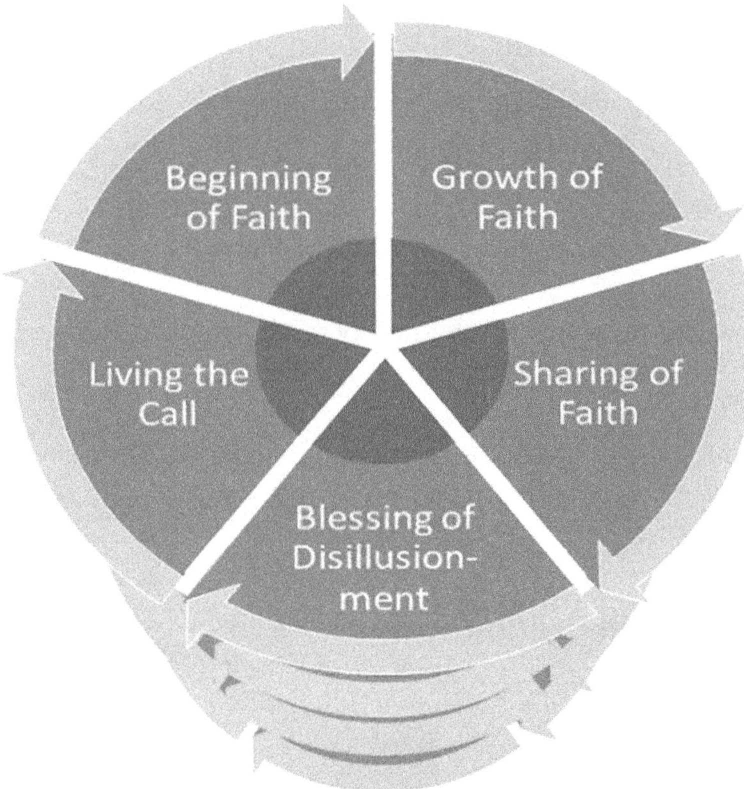

Chapter 9 Leadership Reflection:

Character of the Leader

Consider the following verses in view of what has been presented in the readings and in the greater context of each verse. Let the Holy Spirit guide your reading.

> *It shall not be so among you. But whoever would be great among you must be your servant.* (Matthew 20:26 ESV)

> *He must increase, but I must decrease.* (John 3:30 ESV)
>
> *Do nothing from selfish ambition or conceit, but in humility count others more significant than yourselves.* (Philippians 2:3 ESV)

Personal Reflection:

- What does it mean to be a successful leader in the eyes of God?

- How does the character of humility mesh with the concept of a visionary leader?

Leadership Reflection Two:

Shepherding the Flock

> *Know well the condition of your flocks, and give attention to your herds* (Proverbs 27:23 ESV)

- How might leading with a view to the stages of faith development apply to this verse?

- Consider those in the flock entrusted to your care. Which stages of faith are they in? How might you readjust your leadership vision to accommodate their stages and to facilitate further growth?

Final Reflection:

> *Commit your way to the Lord; trust in him, and he will act.* (Psalm 37:5 ESV)

- As you consider this verse, think about what allowing God to lead would look like in your church. How can His leadership be communicated to your members?

References

Allender, D. B. *Leading with a Limp.* Colorado Springs: WaterBrook Press, 2006.

Anderson, R. S. *The Soul of Ministry.* Louisville: Westminister John Knox Press, 1997.

Calhoun, A. A. *Spiriutal Disciplines Handbook: Practices that Transform Us.* Downers Grove: InterVarsity Press, 2005.

Crabb, L. *Becoming a True Spiritual Community: A Profound Vision of What the Church Can Be.* Nashville: Thomas Nelson, 1999.

Crabb, L. *Safest Place on Earth: Where people Connect and are Forever Changed.* Nashville: W Publishing Group, 1999.

Demarest, B. *Seasons of the Soul.* Downers Grove: InterVarsity Press, 2009.

Foster, R. *Celebration of Discipline.* San Francisco: HarperSanFrancisco, 1988.

Fowler, J. W. *Stagesof Faith:The Psychology Human Development and the Quest for Meaning.* New York: HarperCollins, 1981.

Green, T. H. *When the Well Runs dry: Prayer Beyond the Beginnings.* Notre Dame: Ave Maria Press, 2007.

Groeschel, B. *Spiritual Passages: The Psychology of Spiritual Development.* New York: The Crossroad Publishing Company, 1999.

Guiness, O. *God in the Dark: The Assurance of Faith Beyond a Shadow of Doubt.* Wheaton: Crossways Books, 1996.

Hagberg, J. O. and Guelich, R. A. *The Critical Journey.* Salem: Sheffield Publishing Company, 2005.

Maxwell, J. C. *The 21 Irrefutable Laws of Leadership.* Nashville: Thomas Nelson Publishers, 1998.

Sample, S. B. *The Contrarian's Guide to Leadership.* San Francisco: Jossey-Bass, 2002.

The Holy Bible, English Standard Version (ESV). Wheaton: Crossway, 2001.

The Holy Bible, New International Version (NIV). Colorado Springs: International Bible Society, 1978.

Thomas, G. *Thirsting for God*. Eugene: Harvest House Publishers, 2001.

Uniquely You. (n.d.) Retrieved from Uniquely You: http://www.uniquelyyou.org

Willard, D. *The Spirit of the Disciplines: Understanding How God Changes Lives.* San Francisco: HarperSanFrancisco, 1988.

Appendix A: Old Testament Journeys of Sanctification

Seasons	The Sanctifying Journey of the Kings			
	Solomon's Prayer	Asa	Hezekiah	Josiah
Season 1 Humility (Seeking)	2 Chr 6:22–23	2 Chr 14:2	2 Chr 29:2, 10, 19–20	2 Chr 34:2–3
Season 2 Repentant Heart	2 Chr 6:24, 37–39	2 Chr 14:3–5	2 Chr 29:14	2 Chr 34:3–8
Season 3 Consecration (Sacrifice)	2 Chr 6:25	2 Chr 14:6–7	2 Chr 29:12, 15	2 Chr 34:8–17
Season 4 Tested Heart	2 Chr 6:26	2 Chr 15:1–6	2 Chr 32:31	
Season 5 Dedication, Praise	2 Chr 6:27	2 Chr 15:8–11	2 Chr 29:19–20	
Season 6 Examination	2 Chr 6:28	2 Chr 15:7–8	2 Chr 31:1, 5	2 Chr 34:18–27
Season 7 Covenanting Proclamation	2 Chr 6:30–35	2 Chr 15:9–15	2 Chr 29:31, 30:5, 31:2	2 Chr 34:29–32
Season 8 Captive Heart	2 Chr 6:36	2 Chr 16:1–14	2 Chr 32:25–26	2 Chr 34:24–25
Season 9 Sanctification (Completion)	2 Chr 6:40–41	2 Chr 15:15–19	2 Chr 32–33	2 Chr 34:28, 33

Appendix B: The Authenticity of Asaph and His Journey through Disillusionment

Psalm 73:1–28 (NIV)

Consider the following scriptures:

> *Surely God is good to Israel, to those who are pure in heart.*

In this verse, Asaph (King David's praise team leader) brings the focus right to front and center, proclaiming the goodness of God!

When we go there (like Asaph), and actually acknowledge the depth of the goodness that God brings and acknowledge that He is the ONLY One that IS good, if we move forward in an honest and authentic way, we begin the journey down the road that leads toward the "blessing of disillusionment."

The second half of this verse leaves one with a question that begs asking: If God is the only One who brings good and IS good, then who of us is pure in heart?

Continuing down the path with Asaph:

> *But as for me, my feet had almost slipped; I had nearly lost my foothold.*
> *For I envied the arrogant when I saw the prosperity of the wicked.*

Here we find that Asaph acknowledged the depth of his ongoing struggle.

He also acknowledged his oppression at a heart level by defining his challenge and uncovering the emotional layers that lay under his frustration ("*envied the arrogant*"). This is vital!

He goes on to write of his frustration (most likely built up over years):

> *They have no struggles; their bodies are healthy and strong.*
> *They are free from the burdens common to man; they are*

not plagued by human ills.
Therefore pride is their necklace; they clothe themselves with violence.
From their callous hearts comes iniquity; the evil conceits of their minds know no limits.
They scoff, and speak with malice; in their arrogance they threaten oppression.
Their mouths lay claim to heaven, and their tongues take possession of the earth.
Therefore their people turn to them and drink up waters in abundance.
They say, "How can God know? Does the Most High have knowledge?"
This is what the wicked are like—always carefree, they increase in wealth.

We too can express our frustrations and complaints to God about his creation (as David also did).

The important part is to get the frustration, complaints, and especially the underlying emotional passion and beliefs down in writing. It is essential to define the emotional content and beliefs that lie underneath the frustration.

Again, it is most helpful to write this out as David, a man after God's own heart, also did. The pages can be written in a journal, can be shared with a Christian counselor or mentor, or the writings do not have to be kept.

Consider that this can free us from complaining to one another and might actually move us to a new perspective as we will see later on in this message.

Below, Asaph digs into the disillusionment he was experiencing:

Surely in vain have I kept my heart pure; in vain have I washed my hands in innocence.
All day long I have been plagued; I have been punished every morning.
If I had said, "I will speak thus," I would have betrayed your children.
When I tried to understand all this, it was oppressive to me

Here we see the height of the wall of disillusionment that Asaph was stuck behind and the depth of the ongoing oppression that he was experiencing.

Note that he described it with emotional fluency: "*plagued . . . punished . . . unable to understand . . . it was oppressive to me.*"

The sense of being weighed down by oppression is a clear clue that one might be in the stage of "the blessing of disillusionment." That's right! This disillusionment can lead to blessing!

Now we read of Asaph taking his burden to God:

> *Till I entered the sanctuary of God; then I understood their final destiny.*
> *Surely you place them on slippery ground; you cast them down to ruin.*
> *How suddenly are they destroyed, completely swept away by terrors!*
> *As a dream when one awakes, so when you arise, O LORD, you will despise them as fantasies.*

Here Asaph describes his sense of unworthiness as he comes up against the perfection of God:

> *When my heart was grieved and my spirit embittered,*
> *I was senseless and ignorant; I was a brute beast before you.*

Asaph records his experience of entering God's sanctuary with his burden in authenticity and openness.

He approached God from behind this wall of disillusionment that realistically had been keeping God at a distance.

God took away Asaph's blinders and revealed the reality of the situation. He revealed what Asaph did not understand.

Asaph closes with this praise to God.

> *Yet I am always with you; you hold me by my right hand.*
> *You guide me with your counsel, and afterward you will take me into glory.*
> *Whom have I in heaven but you? And earth has nothing I desire besides you.*
> *My flesh and my heart may fail, but God is the strength of my heart and my portion forever.*
> *Those who are far from you will perish; you destroy all who are unfaithful to you.*
> *But as for me, it is good to be near God. I have made the Sovereign* LORD *my refuge; I will tell of all your deeds.*

And here we find the "blessing," the blessing of the stage of disillusionment!

Appendix C: Journey of Surrender: Confession and Forgiveness

(We advise working through this with a spiritual advisor or a counselor, as he or she can help with processing strong emotions and provide some objectivity that is needed at times.)

1. Write down what you desire for the ideal you, your ideal relationship, and your ideal life situation. Identify where you have made gains and where you have lost ground.

2. Process your life journey to this point. List your life losses/hurts/failures and gains/pleasures/successes that you have had, laying them out in five- to ten-year segments. Start at age 0. Leave some extra space after each segment.

3. Go through each segment listed and take note of the thoughts (beliefs) that you took hold of in these experiences. Share these beliefs with God. As you sense the presence of Christ in your memory, what would He say about these beliefs? Write down both the thoughts/beliefs and what you have gained from Christ's perspective.

4. Go through every experience and note the feelings that are left over from each. What are the longings underneath the feelings? Tell God your longings. Listen to His response.

5. Go through each experience and note any need for confession or forgiveness. This could include forgiveness of self, others, your environment, or even God. When you are ready, go through your list and confess or forgive anything needed before God. As you address each of these, imagine that each thing on your list is nailed to the cross.

6. Confess to God that your insistence on obtaining the longings of your heart may have gotten in the way of seeking God's desires and purposes for your life. Receive His forgiveness and be open to allow God to continue to heal your heart.

7. Focus your heart on Jesus and His gift of forgiveness. Praise God for this gift and ask Him to reveal to you how you might best live out what He has made available to you.

Appendix D: Using This Book with Leadership Teams

This book is primarily designed to be used by an individual leader. However, we do recognize that some leaders will want to gather their teams and walk through this together with a view to discovering how it might fit into their churches. We applaud this approach and have a few thoughts on how it might best be used for this purpose.

We feel that before one can really apply the principles of this book well, the whole of the faith journey needs to be grasped. Therefore, we advise holding off on discussions on how it might look in the church until the Chapter 9 discussions.

As the material is intended to help individuals deepen their walk with God, we feel an adequate amount of soak time for each chapter is a key component. Our recommendation is to allow each chapter a month of this soak time. This would make walking through the book together a nine-month to one-year project. A leadership retreat might be a good option for the questions added below for Chapter 9.

An outline of a possible walk with a leadership team follows:

I. Read Chapters 1 through 8 individually and work through the reflections. Meet as a group after each chapter and discuss appropriate parts of those individual reflections. Hold any attempts to assign stages to self or others very loosely during this time; it may change as you progress through the book.

II. Read Chapter 9 individually and process the reflections. As a group, discuss the reflections and **add the following questions**:

    A. What friends or acquaintances do you believe are living out the call (Stage 5)? How might we better engage their wisdom?

    B. Beginning of faith (Stage 1) considerations:

        i. What passions do we see in those who are in the sharing of faith stage (Stage 3) and those in Stage 5 who might help set up the healing ministries needed for those in the beginning of faith (Stage 1)?

- **ii.** What ministries are offered by others in our community that we can endorse?
- **iii.** How can we engage the enthusiasm of this group in other areas of ministry?

C. Growth of faith (Stage 2) considerations:

- **i.** Are there any of our current educational programs for those in the growth of faith stage that need to be modified?
    - **a.** Any that need to be started?
    - **b.** Any that need to be jettisoned?
- **ii.** Are the programs led by qualified Stages 3 and 5 leaders?
- **iii.** Are there other programs in the community we can endorse?
- **iv.** Are we looking for opportunities to assign Stage 2 members as apprentices to the ministries we have?

D. How well are we doing at modeling the principle of unity (Matthew 18)?

- **i.** Do we watch for divisiveness in the Body and proactively address it?
- **ii.** Do we regularly communicate the need for grace in the Body?
- **iii.** Do we need to start with *this* team?

E. Sharing of faith (Stage 3) considerations

- **i.** Are our sharing of faith ministries aligned with the Great Commission?
- **ii.** What adjustments might be needed?

F. Blessing of disillusionment (Stage 4) considerations

- **i.** Who do we see that might serve as mentors for those in the blessing of disillusionment?
- **ii.** How might we better empower them to serve in this way?

G. Are we mindful of transitioning members of the Body (moving from one stage to the next) and ready to assist?

About the Authors

Let us introduce ourselves. I am Michael, the primary writer of the contents of each chapter, though Valerie has collaborated with me in this and has written much of the reflective practices that conclude each chapter. There has been a synergistic dynamic between God, Valerie, and me over the course of the 30-some years of our Christian lives together, and much of what will be shared in this book cannot be called mine, or even ours, as it has come about through much discerning prayer, many deep conversations, and the sharing of many outside sources as they have touched each of us. For these reasons, I will use the pronoun "we" most often when I write about the ideas that we have found helpful in leading our church.

Since so many are concerned about qualifications, it is appropriate to share that I have several degrees: Doctor of Education in Counseling Psychology (Argosy University/American School of Psychology), a Master of Arts in Educational Ministries (Wheaton College), and a Bachelor of Arts in Religious Studies (Concordia University College of Alberta). I also have about a year of seminary coursework in theological topics (Concordia Lutheran Seminary, Alberta). I have served as an associate pastor and core leadership team member in a growing suburban church (14 years), and concurrently as a founder/director of a nonprofit Christian counseling center (12 years), in paid mission field leadership in Russia (3 years), and in lay leadership capacities in the Church (2 years). Most recently, I have served on the leadership and prayer team of a small-town church for several years as the church negotiated some very difficult times. These venues are the ones that have given me an avenue to grow and learn about Christian leadership.

In addition, I am an adjunct professor at the graduate and undergraduate level of Liberty University and have worked in that capacity for over 10 years. It is my privilege to serve students with an emphasis on the Biblical perspective.

Prior to this time, I spent a 20-year career working in the nuclear power industry in a number of leadership roles. After working my way up through the ranks of operations, I obtained and held a senior reactor operator's license, allowing me to supervise the operations of a commercial nuclear power plant. Later, I was certified as a project engineer and led several extremely profitable projects through the development of some very high performing teams, and I finally served as a corporate training manager, leading the collective training efforts for licensed operators in all the nuclear plants of the Tennessee Valley Authority.

Valerie and I have been married for over 35 years. Five years into our marriage, Jesus introduced Himself to me, and Valerie and I became fully dedicated followers and gave our lives to serving Him. An essential for us, as was Christ's custom, is getting away for times of resting, regenerating, and seeking direction in quiet places. Most often, we follow rhythms of quarterly retreats for quiet Bible meditation and journaling for two to three days at a time.

Valerie is the author of the spiritual practices that complete each chapter. She is uniquely shaped by God to engage in this endeavor. She has completed Doctor of Ministry studies in Spiritual Transformation from Northern Theological Seminary (Certificate in Spiritual Transformation: A Two-Year Experience of Spiritual Formation for Leaders, issued by the Transforming Center) and is a certified spiritual director through the Christos Center for Spiritual Formation. It has also been her privilege to have attended Larry Crabb's School of Spiritual Direction. Valerie has a Master of Divinity equivalency from Northern Theological Seminary, a Master of Arts in Clinical Psychology from Wheaton College, and a Bachelor of Science degree in Human Resource Administration from Mercer University.

Valerie has served on the Spirituality Committee for the Society for Christian Psychology and been a spiritual director for their conferences. Valerie has also authored articles in *Soul and Spirit,* a quarterly publication of the Society. She is a licensed clinical professional counselor, and is the founder of Foundation Counseling and Training. In addition, she worked in the business world for over 13 years.

Most importantly, Valerie is a lifelong Christian who has pursued God from her heart. It has been her privilege to have read through the Bible over 17 times, and she continues but stopped counting because it has simply become lifeblood to her. She has also served in key church lay leadership capacities throughout the last 30 years, with the main focus of her ministry as a cofounder, cotrainer, and leader of a Stephen Ministry of 15 years. Her leadership background also includes her role as special events coordinator at a Christian university.

I have had the privilege of living side by side with Valerie and have watched the depth of her commitment to follow Jesus. This has, at times, been in the face of pressure to conform to external expectations and practices that are not in themselves wrong, but are not in conformity with what God was leading her to do. That level of surrender to obedience and listening is alone the greatest qualification I could attest to.

Valerie is also an Adjunct Professor at the undergraduate level in Psychology at Liberty University, where Michael is as well. She is delighted to bring the Biblical perspective and her love for the Lord to encourage her students. She emphasizes and has found in her life experience that: "He is faithful, faithful, faithful!"

I (Valerie) would like to share from my personal experience of my husband.

Over the years, he has worn five different hats on the pastoral staff. He is an inspirational leader and has been considered and sought out as "the wise guy" (not only on staff, in counseling and with theology)! He has served on the senior staff team as executive pastor, small group pastor, children's pastor, and care and counseling pastor of a large and growing church. This includes being the director of a 501(c)3 (nonprofit) professional counseling center to serve the Christian community. By God's grace, I am amazed at his ability to negotiate the many long-term dual relationships, and many of us know how difficult this can be. Mike has a heart to serve wherever he is needed.

His leadership has included years of team development of church staff, as well as answering the tough questions from new members and indepth Bible-in-a-year classes. Mike has led his own "mini-care ministry church" in the "barn" at our large campus. He has led multiple lay-level Bible studies that expound the full richness of Scripture, from the mission field in Russia leading both college students and retired volunteers, to working with the indigenous church in evangelistic efforts.

Mike has also been involved with interchurch exchanges and has counseled challenged pastors and members from multiple church settings. He is currently mentoring a number of up-and-coming young men involving their call to ministry education and roles. As you can tell, my respect for my husband's leadership gifts runs deep.

Together we have had the opportunity to present workshops and seminars, both as a couple and individually, at venues that include the American Association of Christian Counselors, the Society for Christian Psychology, the Christian Association for Psychological Studies, the Illinois Association of Marriage and Family Therapists, and various church presentations, both local and international. We have also had the privilege of working with the Counseling Network of the European Leadership Forum, serving as mentors and idea generators. Through the grace of God, our lives have been full and blessed with opportunity.

Our prayer is that this book will open up new avenues of thought about leadership and begin a conversation that leads to a healthier Body of Christ.

Printed in the USA
CPSIA information can be obtained
at www.ICGtesting.com
LVHW050726120124
768730LV00003B/303